Bluebirds Forever

Connie Toops

VOYAGEUR PRESS

Edited by Elizabeth Knight
Designed by Lou Gordon and Kathryn Mallien
Bluebird nest box drawings by Andrea Rud
Printed in China
95 96 97 98 5 4 3 2

Library of Congress Cataloging-in-Publication Data
Toops, Connie M.
Bluebirds forever / by Connie Toops.
            p.   cm.
Includes bibliographical references and index.
ISBN 0-89658-249-3
1. Bluebirds. 2. Bird attracting. I. Title.
QL696.P288T66   1994
598.8'42 — dc20   94–11710
                                                   CIP

Distributed in Canada by Raincoast Books, 112 East Third Avenue, Vancouver, B.C. V5T 1C8

Published by Voyageur Press, Inc.
123 North Second Street, P.O. Box 338, Stillwater, MN 55082 U.S.A.
612-430-2210, fax 612-430-2211

Please write or call, or stop by, for our free catalog of natural history publications. Our toll-free
number to place an order or to obtain a free catalog is 800-888-WOLF (800-888-9653).

Educators, fundraisers, premium and gift buyers, publicists, and marketing managers: Looking for
creative products and new sales ideas? Voyageur Press books are available at special discounts
when purchased in quantities, and special editions can be created to your specifications.
For details contact our marketing department.

Page 1: *Male eastern bluebird offering a mulberry to its mate. (Photo copyright by Connie Toops)* Page 3: *Male mountain bluebird. (Photo copyright by Willard E. Dilley)* Page 4: *Male mountain bluebirds in a late spring snowstorm. (Photo copyright by Glenn Van Nimwegen)*

Acknowledgments

The author wishes to thank the following individuals and organizations, who provided information, access to bluebird nest boxes, or other assistance in preparing this book:

Dave and Jan Ahlgren, Helene Anderson, Antietam National Battlefield, Audubon Society of Corvallis, Audubon Society of Portland, Art Aylesworth, Beaverhead National Forest, Beltsville Agricultural Research Center, Bluebird Recovery Program (Audubon Chapter of Minneapolis), Delaware State Park, Elsie Eltzroth, W.L. Finley National Wildlife Refuge, Frederick County Park and Recreation District, Steve Gilbertson, Earl Gillis, Jim and Janet Harvey, Jean Horton, Joe Huber, Barney Hudson, Lynn Husband, Mary Janetatos, Linda Janilla, Pat Johnston, Berlin Kauffman, Ron Kingston, Elizabeth Knight, Ken Lightle, Kathy Mallien, Martinsburg Public Library, Renee Mason, Terry McEneaney, Mary McGee, Brenda McGowan, Minnesota Department of Natural Resources Nongame Wildlife Program, Mountain Bluebird Trails, Tom and Tammy Mizik, Betty Nichols, North American Bluebird Society, Ohio Department of Natural Resources, Tommy Outerbridge, Steve Packard, Patuxent National Wildlife Refuge Research Library, Myrna Pearman, Scott Peavy, Al Perry, Bruce Peterjohn, Dick Peterson, Harry Power, Hubert Prescott Western Bluebird Recovery Project, Mark and Jean Raabe, Robert and Lois Rager, William Read, Jo Riggs, Andrea Rud, Dorene Scriven, Pat Toops, Richard Tuttle, Tom Valega, John White, Stephanie Wood, Larry Zeleny.

Bluebird survival depends upon compassionate human hosts.
This book is dedicated to all of you, whether you tend one bluebird nest
box or a hundred. You have discovered the joy of bluebirds,
and you willingly share this magic with others.

Contents

Anticipation

When we moved into our new home in West Virginia a year ago, the yard was strewn with broken bricks and piles of rocky fill dirt. The view from my office window scarcely resembled a wildlife haven, so imagine my delight when a puff of blue and orange caught my eye! A male bluebird perched in the bare elm tree, embellishing the winter-weary landscape. Quietly, unassertively, he scanned the barren ground.

"Little bluebird," I wondered, "how can I let you know we'll salvage this muddy mess? We'll build nest boxes and a birdbath. We'll grow plants you'll like for winter food."

His sharp eyes zeroed in, and he flew to a scrawny tree the bulldozer had missed. Balancing on a swaying limb, the bluebird stretched and plucked something from the branch above. A few moments later he repeated the harvesting maneuver. Then he wheeled away over the roof.

This blustery February morning was too chilly for insects to be active. Curiosity aroused, I walked outside to inspect the tree where the bluebird had lingered. I found small orange fruits dangling from the limbs. The sapling was a sugarberry.

During the next week the bluebird returned each day, sometimes with one or two females. They seemed happy with each other's company, behaving more like a family than a love triangle. They twittered softly to each other as they fluttered from branch to branch, taking turns plucking sugarberries. They stayed only a few minutes during each visit, then continued their neighborhood rounds.

As soon as the ground thawed, we installed two nest boxes. We were thrilled when a pair of tree swallows showed interest in one and bluebirds carried bits of grass into the other. But house wrens eventually won both. The bluebirds did remain in the neighborhood, however, choosing a box in a spacious yard four blocks away.

During the summer they perched on utility lines and scanned grassy lawns for insects. They raised two broods and by August were feeding in a wider radius. We heard them fly overhead. "Chee-do," they called, keeping the family together, "chee-do."

Were they noticing the open lawn we left on the south side of the house? Had they taken note of the berry-laden poke growing at the edge of the yard? Did they see the wild grapes, dogwood, sugarberries, and hackberries waiting to sustain them through the winter? Maybe our birdbath or the birdhouse relocated near the driveway caught their eyes.

Another brutal winter is passing, and I marvel as the bluebirds survive bout after bout of ice and snow. Frequently I glance out the window to see a male and female peeking into our nest boxes. This winter they have relied upon our hackberries. They leisurely consume a fruit or two, sit and preen while they digest, then spit out the large, hard seeds. After a few

Opposite: "*If the warble of the first bluebird does not thrill you, know that the morning and spring of your life are past.*" —*Henry David Thoreau. (Male eastern bluebird, photo copyright by Gregory K. Scott) Above: Female eastern bluebird. (Photo copyright by Connie Toops)*

Soon after we moved, we began landscaping the yard of our new home to attract wildlife. Now, when I glance out my office window, I am often rewarded with the sight of an eastern bluebird balanced on a swaying limb. (Photo copyright by Connie Toops)

berries, they fly to the water, where as many as five have gathered, shoulder to shoulder around the dish, as they quench their thirst.

Will they raise a family near our doorstep in the spring? Anticipation is a big part of bluebirding. We watch and listen with hope.

❧

In writing about nature and wildlife, there is sometimes a tendency to anthropomorphize—to attribute human qualities to animals. But students of science in its purest form draw conclusions from statistics. They document how many times per hour a courting male sings or the number of feeding visits parents make to their nestlings. They divorce themselves from observations that suggest animals are capable of thought or emotion.

Those of us caught up in the lives of bluebirds may become so familiar with "our" birds that we be-lieve otherwise. Birding expert Roger Tory Peterson agrees there is validity in this latter point of view. Peterson believes some birds—such as the chicka-dees that visit our feeders or the bluebirds that grace our yards—have lost a bit of their fear of being around humans. He thinks they may somehow real-ize we help them survive.

❧

Understanding nature is not a simple task. We may never know the answers to some natural history ques-tions or the reasons for certain behaviors. In learn-ing about bluebirds, we discover nothing about them should be taken for granted. For everything we think we know, someone will find an exception.

Could that be the underlying reason for our love affair with these delightful birds? They seem so will-ing to share their lives with us, yet they always hold a few surprises in store.

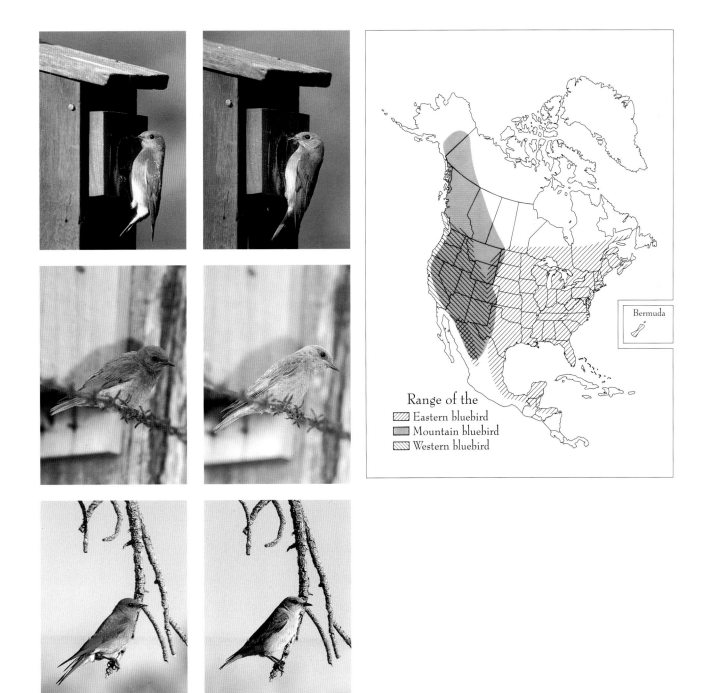

Top row: *Male (left) and female (right) eastern bluebirds. (Both photos copyright by Paul Zimmerman)* Center row: *Male (left) and female (right) western bluebirds. (Both photos copyright by Connie Toops)* Bottom row: *Male (left) and female (right) mountain bluebirds. (Both photos copyright by Connie Toops)*

Blue Robins

As colonists began to settle North America, their friends, relatives, and sponsors in Europe hungered for descriptions of this unknown land and the wild creatures that occupied it. English artist Mark Catesby traveled to Williamsburg, Virginia, in 1712. Enthralled by the flora and fauna, he remained for seven years, roaming the countryside with his journals and paints. Catesby returned to eastern North America in 1722 for another four years of observations. His resulting two-volume *Natural History of Carolina, Florida and the Bahama Islands* contained 220 wildlife portraits.

Catesby laid the groundwork for American ornithology. His books included 113 bird paintings. Two-thirds were species new to science. One of Catesby's plates is titled "The Blew Bird." His accompanying text described them as sparrow-sized, with large eyes. "They make their nests in holes of trees, are harmless birds, and resemble our robin-redbreast," Catesby observed.

One of the familiar backyard birds of the Old World is the European robin. Slightly smaller than the eastern bluebird but similar in shape and breast color, European robins have brown backs. When colonists noticed gentle blue birds with russet breasts in their gardens, they called them "blue robins." The resemblance is not mere coincidence, for European robins and North American bluebirds are members of *Turdidae*, the thrush family. It includes more than three hundred species worldwide. There are two dozen representatives in Europe and eleven in North America. The most widespread and abundant in the United States and Canada is the American robin. The group also includes veeries, along with wood, hermit, Swainson's, and gray-cheeked thrushes. All are drab birds of the forest understory with pleasant, flutelike voices. Varied thrushes, robin lookalikes with dark breast bands, inhabit moist Pacific Northwest forests. Townsend's solitaires range throughout the western mountains. They are slender, and like flycatchers, they flit from treetop perches to catch passing insects. Rounding out the North American thrushes are eastern, western, and mountain bluebirds.

Ornithologists have identified approximately nine thousand species of birds in the world. They are categorized into 170 families, such as *Turdidae*. In each family, birds closely related by physical and genetic characteristics are placed within the same genus. *Sialia*, a name derived from Greek, meaning "a kind of bird," is the genus name for bluebirds. Paleontologists hypothesize that ancestral songbirds evolved about thirty million years ago. Occupying habitats from forest canopy to understory allowed them to diversify into families such as thrushes, vireos, warblers, and sparrows. The qualities that make all thrushes kin include five- to nine-inch (13- to 23-cm) size, earth-toned colors (many with spotted breasts), and narrow bills useful for catching small insects or eating fleshy berries. They feed by hop-

Female eastern bluebird feeding babies. (Photo copyright by Michael L. Smith)

Early settlers in North America called bluebirds "blue robins" because they resembled European robins, which are familiar backyard birds in the Old World. The American robin, perched here next to a western bluebird, is much larger than the European species. (Photo copyright by Connie Toops)

ping on the ground or dropping to the ground from a low perch. Many thrushes nest in temperate areas and migrate to warmer climates for the winter.

Biochemists have analyzed tissue samples from seven North American thrushes to determine their evolutionary relationships. As could be expected from their similar outward appearances, veeries and hermit, Swainson's, and gray-cheeked thrushes have a very similar genetic heritage. Wood thrushes are "cousins." American robins are more distantly related to the spot-breasted thrushes. The genetic characteristics of bluebirds fall between those of robins and wood thrushes. It is unclear whether robins and bluebirds derived from a common ancestor or whether each branched from the thrush line and developed independently.

≈

Bluebirds live solely in the Western Hemisphere. Of the 650 bird species that breed in North America, there are only three types of bluebirds. Eastern bluebirds (*Sialia sialis*) occur east of the Rocky Mountains. In summer they venture as far north as southern Quebec, Ontario, and Manitoba to nest. They winter in the southeastern and south-central United States,

with some individuals migrating along the east coast of Mexico into Belize, northern Honduras, Guatemala, and the pinelands of Nicaragua. A few eastern bluebirds overwinter in the Bahamas and western Cuba. A small resident population inhabits the island of Bermuda.

Throughout most of their range, male eastern bluebirds are distinguished by cobalt blue plumage on the head, back, wings, and tail. The throat, breast, and flank feathers are a cinnamon orange color, with white on the belly and undertail coverts. A distinct, nonmigratory subspecies occurs in southeastern Arizona and south into Mexico. It was once considered a separate species, the azure bluebird. These males are lighter blue with more pure orange tones on the breast.

Female plumage of all three species is less flashy but patterned similarly to the male's. Female eastern bluebirds are blue-gray on the head and back. Feathers in the wings and tail are less brilliant cobalt blue. They have a dull orange throat and breast, with dingy white belly and undertail coverts.

Western bluebirds (*Sialia mexicana*) reside from the Rocky Mountains to the West Coast. Their range extends from southern British Columbia to central

Mexico. Male western bluebirds wear plumage of deep ultramarine blue on the head, back, wings, tail, and throat. In some males, blue extends down the center of the breast to the upper belly. Auburn orange feathers decorate the breast and the flanks and, in many individuals, form a rusty patch above the shoulder. The belly and undertail coverts are grayish white. Female western bluebirds have gray-brown plumage on the head, back, and throat. Their wing and tail feathers are azure blue, shaded with gray. Breast feathers are chestnut orange.

As the older names "Arctic" and "Rocky Mountain" bluebird imply, mountain bluebirds (*Sialia currucoides*) inhabit higher and colder terrain than do the other two species. They ply the western mountains, spilling onto the Great Basin, the northwestern Great Plains, and Canada's Prairie Provinces. They nest as far north as central Saskatchewan, Alberta, northern British Columbia, and southeastern Alaska. They range south into central Mexico.

Male mountain bluebirds are cerulean blue on the head, back, wings, and tail. The throat and breast are blue-gray, and undertail coverts are white. Females have a gray head, back, throat, and breast. After molting, females show a buffy orange tint on the throat and chest. Their wing and tail feathers are blue shaded with gray.

Juvenile birds of all three species look very similar. They have gray-brown plumage on the head and back. The breast and shoulders are gray, speckled with white. The belly and undertail coverts are gray. Youngsters develop white eye rings. By the time they fledge, males can be distinguished from females by richer blue color in the wing and tail feathers.

A few mountain bluebirds wander as far east as Iowa, Minnesota, and Wisconsin, and eastern bluebirds trickle west to southeastern Saskatchewan, eastern Montana, and eastern Wyoming. In several instances, usually at the extremes of the two species' ranges, nests in which one parent is a mountain bluebird and the other is an eastern bluebird are known. These occur most often in southern portions of Canada's Prairie Provinces, and hybrid eggs do hatch.

Although mountain bluebirds and western bluebirds share more overlapping territory, they do not readily hybridize. The first report of such a union was in western Montana in 1987. A male western blue-

bird and a female mountain bluebird successfully raised six young. When they left the nest, the banded hybrid fledglings were otherwise indistinguishable from young western and mountain bluebirds in the area. Eastern and western bluebirds overlap in so little area that, so far, no hybrid pairings are known.

❧

Bluebirds belong to the order of perching birds known as *Passeriformes*. This is a huge group, containing more than half of the world's bird species. Most have a well-developed syrinx, or voice box, and thus are commonly called "songbirds." Their form is compact and balanced so the center of gravity is directly over the legs and feet when perched. Three toes point forward and one points to the rear, an arrangement that makes it easy to land on and grasp tree branches. A tail consisting of a dozen feathers provides stability in flight. The wings of passerine birds are relatively short. They are wider at the base, tapering to an elliptical tip. This design allows rapid takeoffs and agile, twisting flight. Most songbirds possess ten strong primary feathers in each wing. Primaries reach to their fullest extent as the wings stroke through the air, providing the propulsion for flight. Broad secondary feathers, attached between the elbow and the shoulder, are cambered, like the wing of an airplane, so that air takes longer to cross the convex top surface than it does to rush underneath. This differential produces the lift necessary to keep a bird in flight. To reduce weight, birds' bones are hollow or paper-thin. Load-bearing bones are reinforced by struts inside their hollow cores.

Feathers take several forms. Large vaned feathers compose the wings and tail. Several hundred parallel filaments, called barbs, attach to opposing sides of the shaft. They are held together by barbules, microscopic hooks that interlock the filaments while allowing them to flex in flight. Down and semiplume feathers do not interlock. They fill in beneath contour feathers, next to the skin, where they fluff to form a layer of insulation.

Songbirds the size of bluebirds typically have about 2,500 feathers. Feather density is greatest in the fall, after bluebirds molt. By the following summer, a third of the feather mass is lost as tips and edges wear.

The blueness of bluebirds is a distinctive feature, since blue feathers are found on only 2 percent of North American species. In the mid-1800s, naturalist Henry David Thoreau described the color, writing, "The bluebird carries the sky on his back."

Navajo Indians of the American Southwest considered this sky-blue color sacred. Pimas were also fascinated with the color. According to one of their legends, the male mountain bluebird originally was dull gray, similar to the female. Then an ancestral bird bathed in a unique lake that had neither inlet nor outlet. When it emerged, the bluebird's feathers were the same cerulean blue as the sky.

With the aid of powerful microscopes, physicists can explain why the color of a bluebird is so stunning. Birds that are black, gray, and brown, and some that are yellow, have colors produced by minute melanin particles. Red, orange, and other shades of yellow are carotenoids, color granules diffused in tiny droplets of fat. These pigments are located within the feather barbs and barbules. When light strikes them, they absorb all other color wavelengths, reflecting only the hue of the pigment.

There is no blue pigment in bluebird feathers. Like the shimmering colors of a soap bubble, the blue originates from light waves scattered by a unique structure in the feather. A cross-section of a barb from a bluebird feather, when viewed under a microscope, reveals dark pigment sandwiched between two layers of hollow-cored tubular cells. When light rays strike the feather, most wavelengths are absorbed by the dark pigment. The hollow, transparent cells scatter the few wavelengths of light that are not absorbed, and they emerge from the feather looking blue. The intensity of blue depends upon the brightness and angle of the sunlight illuminating the feather. Thus a bluebird may look deeper blue at midday in full sun than at dawn or on a cloudy day. In a sense, the blue color is an optical illusion.

❧

A century ago, bluebirds were almost as common as robins are today. They prospered in rural areas that offered meadows dotted with trees. Our great-grandparents saw them around orchards, gardens, and even in towns where homes and businesses were surrounded by green space.

Open areas are important because during warmer weather bluebirds hunt insects that live in short, sparse grasses. They nest nearby in tree cavities formed naturally by decay or in holes created and later abandoned by woodpeckers. During the winter, bluebirds rely on fruits to supplement their insect diet, and thus spend more time foraging near wooded areas.

Bluebird populations "crash" periodically. These population declines coincide with unusually cold or icy winter weather, when many of the birds starve. Crashes occur every ten to fifteen years, but historically, if succeeding nesting seasons had mild weather, numbers rebounded within three or four years.

Bluebirds prospered as the North American continent was settled. In addition to nesting in tree cavities, they readily moved into holes in wooden fence posts and recesses in log cabins and farm buildings. Clearings for pastures, gardens, and orchards offered additional foraging space. But in the early 1900s, bluebird populations began to decline. So serious was the decrease that when in the middle of this century the New York legislature considered making the eastern bluebird the state bird, one delegate objected. He stated, "I think this is a bit premature. After all, who has ever seen a bluebird, except perhaps on the cover of a greeting card?"

Foremost among the multiple reasons for bluebird scarcity were decreasing habitat and nest site competition from two nonnative birds, the European starling and the house sparrow, introduced on this continent more than a century ago. Both have spread ubiquitously throughout North America.

Fortunately, a few concerned bird-lovers realized that bluebirds were being ousted from traditional nesting sites. These individuals fashioned wooden nest boxes, which they mounted in areas where isolated populations of bluebirds remained. The birds prospered slowly at first, but as word of successes spread, more people began tending bluebird nest boxes. Now most states, the southern tier of Canadian provinces, and even the island of Bermuda have networks of nest boxes, known as bluebird trails. Perhaps more than any other threatened species of wildlife, bluebirds owe their existence to backyard birders across the continent who refused to allow these sweet "blue robins" to slip into oblivion.

Since blue tones originate when certain wavelengths of light are scattered by special cells within its feathers, the intensity of a bluebird's color varies with the brightness and the angle of light illuminating it. (Photo copyright by Paul Zimmerman)

Bluebird Trails

A Cross-Country Sampler

During the spring and summer of 1993, I visited blue-bird fanciers from Maryland to Oregon. I saw first-hand how bluebird numbers are increasing. I also witnessed the wide variety of foods and housing opportunities offered by human hosts. The settings for these bluebird trails—numbered nest boxes mounted every quarter mile (0.4 km) or so in suitable habitats—varied from backyards and pastoral farmlands to public parks and lonely backcountry rangeland.

Along the way, I pondered why otherwise "normal" people load their vehicles with extra nest boxes, used bluebird nests, hand tools, banding tools, record books, containers of mealworms, and other paraphernalia, then drive for miles along country roads, glancing occasionally at the pavement while intently scanning the fields and fencerows for their beloved bluebirds. You may begin to understand as you follow along on this cross-country tour.

Antietam National Battlefield
Sharpsburg, Maryland

Antietam, a Civil War battlefield, lies in the gentle hills of south-central Maryland. Maintained as a historical park, the landscape resembles the farm clearings and scattered woodlands typical of the mid-1800s. Attorney Mark Raabe and his wife Jean often visit their cabin on Antietam Creek, near the park. In February 1973, they watched with delight as a male eastern bluebird perched on a bare branch outside the cabin window. Mark and Jean grew up in Minnesota, but until that moment, they had never seen a bluebird. Little did they realize the sighting would change their lives.

Mark remembered reading an article about bluebirds by pioneering nest box–maker Larry Zeleny. He called Larry for advice and constructed a nest box that he put up the following weekend. Bluebirds accepted it and raised two broods. During the next few years Mark placed more boxes near the cabin.

Although bluebirds would have been abundant at the time of the Civil War, the battlefield park at Antietam lacked safe nesting sites until Mark Raabe volunteered to install several dozen nest boxes. (Photo copyright by Connie Toops)

In 1978, when Zeleny organized the North American Bluebird Society, he invited Mark to attend. "In that meeting," Raabe recalled, "I listened to descriptions of ideal bluebird habitat and realized I was sitting on a gold mine at Antietam."

Raabe discovered a reference to bluebirds in orchards near Antietam at the time of the Civil War. He met with U. S. National Park Service officials and explained how bluebirds were lacking as a result of limited nest sites and competition from alien house sparrows. Raabe offered to mount cedar nest boxes in unobtrusive locations and monitor them weekly during the nesting season. He began the project in 1979 and currently tends fifty-five boxes on the battlefield plus twenty on private land near his cabin. In an average year, 175 bluebirds fledge from them. Since they began, the Raabes have launched more than two thousand fledglings.

I joined them on a humid July afternoon, as Jean piloted their car past sightseers on the battlefield's narrow roads. At each box, Mark hopped out, opened the lid, and peeked inside. Jean tallied his findings.

A few of the boxes still contained young from first nests, the result of a late, wet spring. Many, however, held fresh nests with eggs of second clutches. Among Mark's discoveries were a former mouse nest with an active bluebird nest on top and a nest with two tree swallows, ready to fledge. Mark cleaned a house sparrow nest from one box and found a male bluebird, pecked to death by a sparrow, in another.

As we passed Bloody Lane, scene of the fiercest Civil War fighting, Mark remarked nests here had been quite successful. "As a matter of fact," he said, "we had an unbelievable event. Two years ago we were check-ing boxes when we came to three in a row that had one more bluebird baby than Jean recorded the previous week." Jean's records showed for June 17, three babies in box 24 and two babies each in boxes 25 and 26. When they checked again on June 25, there were four babies in box 24 and three babies each in boxes 25 and 26.

"I got on her case," Mark admitted, smiling at his wife. "Several months later, I received a letter from Betty Nichols, a bluebirder in Middletown," Raabe continued. "She apologized for the delay, but she wanted to tell me about three orphaned bluebirds from her trail last summer."

Bluebird monitors know if they place orphans with babies of the same age, foster parents often accept and raise them as their own. Mark explained, "Betty couldn't find nests on her trail with similarly aged babies." Boxes 24, 25, and 26 were perfect, and Betty added an orphan to each. "So I did count correctly, and Jean did record the data properly," Mark said, "and Betty's letter solved the mystery."

(In this case, the trail monitor was a skilled rescuer. Anyone faced with a similar dilemma should consult state or federal game officials before relocating eggs or young birds. It is illegal to remove them from nests without permission.)

Mark Raabe checks a bluebird nest box along the trail he maintains at Antietam National Battlefield. (Photo copyright by Connie Toops)

A male eastern bluebird peers into a nest box at Antietam. Since 1979, a restoration project here has fostered more than two thousand young bluebirds.

So Sweet a Song

There are days near the end of a gloomy winter when we yearn for a taste of spring. The sun lingers above the horizon a moment later each evening, and the buds on the maples are swollen. But sharp winds bring low clouds scuttling across the sky, and a skiff of snow covers the dwindling woodpile.

Then we glimpse a splash of color, hunched into the wind, fluffed in its mantle of down. The feathers on its back remind us of the color of the sky on the clearest summer day. Its orange breast seems to radiate warmth from the distant sun. We step onto the deck and hear a soft, lilting warble—a sound that mimics the cadence of a murmuring brook. The bluebird has returned. Can spring be far behind?

The bluebird's presence signals the beginning of an all-important search for suitable nesting space. Migrant males usually arrive several days to a week before the females. They must locate a cavity, then defend it and nearby foraging grounds from competing male bluebirds and other birds who might bully for possession of the chamber. The male bluebird must also entice a female to accept the nest site as her own and himself as a mate.

The beginning of this quest is not so clearly defined in the south, where some bluebirds remain near nesting territories year-round. By returning north before the bluster of winter has fully ended, migrant bluebirds gain a head start of several weeks over competitive swallows and wrens. In the south, eastern bluebirds build nests from late February through mid-March. The onset of breeding activity and nesting occurs about three weeks later with each 10 degrees of latitude farther north. Eastern bluebirds begin nesting in the extreme northern United States and Canada by late April.

In mild areas of the Southwest and along the West Coast, western bluebirds overwinter near, but sometimes at lower elevations than, their summer homes. In Oregon's Willamette Valley, wintering western bluebirds begin courting in March and lay eggs by late March or early April. The arrival dates for migrant western and mountain bluebirds fluctuate, depending upon the severity of the winter. Nesting cannot begin until the snow melts, revealing food and building materials.

Average dates for mountain bluebird nesting are early March in Colorado, mid-March in Alberta and Saskatchewan, and mid-April in Alaska. But migrant mountain bluebirds have been spotted in northern Washington as early as late February. Mountain bluebirds raise two broods in most areas. At extremely high altitudes, they attempt only one brood per season.

Some bluebirds return to the same nest cavity where they were raised. Older, more experienced birds usually stake out the "best" cavities where food is most abundant. Eastern bluebirds use two to three acres (0.8–1.2 hectares) around the nest as a foraging area. Mountain bluebirds require two to five acres (0.8–2 hectares) in which to feed. Younger or later-arriving

Male bluebirds claim nesting territories through a combination of songs and ritualized posturing. (Male eastern bluebird, photo copyright by Paul Zimmerman)

Mountain bluebirds occasionally use abandoned cliff swallow nests if tree cavities are not available. (Photo copyright by Glenn Van Nimwegen)

bluebirds may find cavities they visited the previous year taken, so they search a widening radius. This explains the two- to three-week variation in the onset of spring courtship for older versus inexperienced birds.

Observers around Corvallis, Oregon, documented numerous color-banded western bluebirds returning to their natal boxes. In a study of banded eastern bluebirds in Minnesota, one-quarter to one-third of the adults returned to sites near their previous territories. If bluebirds cannot find nest sites close to their birthplaces, they wander. Most stay within five to ten miles (8–16 km), but a few stray widely. Eastern bluebirds banded as fledglings in Ohio have nested in Alabama and in Michigan. A female banded in Pennsylvania was discovered the following summer on a nest two hundred miles (322 km) northeast in New York.

Bluebirds are inquisitive creatures, and they have occupied a variety of unusual homes. These include newspaper tubes, rural mailboxes, clothespin bags, abandoned cliff swallow nests, crevices in rocks, tin cans, stove pipes, horse trailers, bumpers, grilles, and tailpipes of abandoned cars, and even the empty gas tank of an old tractor.

Good feeding habitat often lacks adequate nesting cavities, so bluebirds are constantly scouting for housing possibilities. Several years ago in the spring, Idaho bluebirder Al Perry was checking a nest box trail that stretches across ninety-five miles (153 km) of the Owyhee Plateau when he noticed a male mountain bluebird on the roof of his car. A female fluttered at the window. In the back seat lay a pile of birdhouses, and Perry realized this pair was interested. He tacked up a box and almost immediately the delighted couple moved in. Since the terrain traversed by Perry's trail is nearly treeless, the octogenarian half-seriously boasts, "I only have to wave a box at a pair flying by to have additional tenants."

Stephanie Wood, a U.S. Forest Service natural resource specialist in Montana, had a similar experience. She was camping in an aspen grove near Virginia City in early April. "I had my boots on top of the car," she recalled, "and a pair of mountain bluebirds began to examine them, looking for a home. I took out some pots and pans, my cook stove, fishing pole carriers, and other camping gear so they could look them over, too. I ended up with four pairs investigating my campsite. That's when I realized cavities were in short supply."

Bluebirds are attracted visually by the contrast of a dark hole against its lighter entrance. Some bluebirders paint decoy holes on the sides of nest boxes to maximize the chances of luring curious passing birds. When investigating a new cavity, a bluebird perches on a branch, rock, or fence post and waits. If nothing has claimed the den, it will flutter in front of the hole or land for a moment and peek in. After poking its head inside several times, the investigator may pop in for a quick look around.

After the male chooses a cavity, he defines the territory around it. This urge results from hormonal responses to lengthening daylight hours. In order to lessen flight weight in nonbreeding seasons, a male bird's sexual organs shrink. When breeding season approaches, hormones secreted by the thyroid gland cause testes to swell two hundred times their off-season size. In bluebirds, the gonads are smaller than a pinhead most of the year, but they enlarge to pea size in the spring. A secondary effect of hormone increases is that males behave more aggressively. Sperm formation also begins.

In female birds, seasonal secretions by the parathyroid gland regulate the amount of calcium in the blood, which affects eggshell formation. Hormones secreted by the pituitary gland prepare the female for incubation. Increased levels of estrogen make her less aggressive and more tolerant of sexual advances by the male.

In nearly all species of North American songbirds, the male proclaims territory through a combination of song and visual communication. The "right" signals—wing and tail movements, plumage adjustments, cocking the head, eye contact, or nuances of song—are too subtle to be judged by humans. But as male bluebirds fly from perch to perch around the boundaries of their territories, females scrutinize them. Bluebirds probably recognize individual voices of other bluebirds and distinguish between them by sight.

Males pause at exposed perches around the perimeter to sing. If a male of a neighboring territory appears, they exchange songs. Each tries to outdo the other's bright beauty and bravado. If an intruder ventures across the boundary, the defender faces his rival, leans forward, and gapes. This signals, in ritualized body language, that the defender will peck or attack the intruder if he persists. If he does, the owner chases him away. More singing—sometimes for as long as fifteen minutes without a significant break—reinforces ownership. Sometimes he sings while flying between perches. As he sings, the male scans the territory to see if any females are listening and watching.

When a male bluebird first proclaims territory, he warbles in his loudest voice. Bluebirds, however, are not noted for forceful songs. Their calls are soft rather than shrill, with only a small pitch range. They are simple and persistent. It is difficult to describe these quavering, melodious jumbles of short syllables with the human voice, but one interpretation of the eastern bluebird's song is "Ayo ala looe? . . . alee lalo looe!" When males first claim territory, they repeat these phrases twenty times per minute.

The territorial displays of eastern, western, and mountain bluebirds are similar, with the exception of song phrases. The tempo of a western bluebird's song is similar to a robin's. The sound is a monotonous "few," or slight variations of that syllable, in rapid phrases. The mountain bluebird's song is a soft, sweet churring, slightly lower pitched than the eastern or western bluebird's. When establishing territories, western and mountain bluebirds are most vocal at dawn.

❧

Once a male attracts a female, he sings more quietly and only half as often as when he was trying to outcompete other males. Focusing his attention on her, the male moves from low perch to low perch, warbling melodic phrases that are seldom heard more than seventy-five feet (23 m) away. The male frequently displays on the wing, banking to one side or slowing his flight until he almost stalls.

When he has the female's undivided attention, he hovers at the entrance to the nest cavity or lands and clings near the hole. Often he carries a bit of nesting material in his bill. He spreads his wings and tail as he pauses there, showing his radiant blue colors to her. He turns and looks over his shoulder, displaying his facial profile. He rocks back and forth, sticking his head and shoulders into the cavity. At last he slips into the den and lingers a moment, sometimes tapping on the sides or floor with his beak. He peeks out the hole, making certain the female sees his face. He may duck into the cavity again or fly out and hover at the entrance. If she continues to watch, he starts another songfest or progresses into stylized courtship displays.

As a genuine pair-bond forms, the male sits at an angle to the female, stretching tall so she can see his sleek, strong profile. If she approaches the cavity, he hunkers down. He spreads his wings and tail to expose their resplendent blues, raising his bill to signal ownership and dominance. If the male wishes to breed, he then bobs up, spreading his wings outward. The female shows her willingness by crouching, with her beak and tail slightly elevated. She opens her wings and lifts her tail higher in readiness for copulation. The male perches beside her, then hops onto her back and nibbles at her head and neck. He presses his tail down next to hers, bringing their cloacal (reproductive chamber) openings into close proximity. Mating is consumated in a few seconds as the male ejects a fine spray containing millions of sperm cells, some of which swim into the female's cloaca and up the oviduct.

Courtship may take a week or two in the spring or less than a day for second and third broods. Throughout most of the male's displays, the female sits impassively on a nearby perch. She notes the radiance of his plumage or the persistence of his song. She may also evaluate whether he has chosen a territory with adequate nesting materials and food supplies. Will his hunting skills support her and a nest of hungry babies? Can he fend away competitors from the nest site? Do his eyes wander toward the female at the box down the fencerow?

We can only guess how she makes her choice. Since older birds pair more quickly, experience must factor into the decision. If the female cannot be enticed into his first cavity, the male leads her on a house-hunting trip. If she is slow to decide, he may again pick up a blade of grass or a pine needle and hover at the entrance to communicate his desire to settle in.

Finally the female enters a cavity and takes a brief look around. The male celebrates with joyful songs and offerings of food. He may even flutter around her in airborne circles. They enter and exit many times, familiarizing themselves with the cavity and its surroundings. Especially if this is the first brood of the season, the couple honeymoons in the territory for about two weeks before constructing a nest.

If a second male arrives, the owner may fly to the cavity or station himself between it and the intruder. He sings as forcefully as a bluebird can. If this does not repel the invader, the owner sounds an alarm, a harsh series of expletive "chuck" or "chup" sounds. Bluebirds are not generally considered ruffians, but if chatter, beak snapping, and dive-bombing flights don't drive the intruder away, the owner lands on his rival's back and pecks at his head and neck while beating him with his wings. Male mountain bluebirds often hover instead of diving at other males. They will face off, rise in flight, lock feet, and tumble to the ground while giving staccato, high-pitched calls.

Fighting males clench in a quivering ball of frenzied wingbeats and roll across the ground, pecking at each other. Disagreements take as long as fifteen minutes to settle, with the less aggressive bird finally being driven away.

During their honeymoon, male and female bluebirds perch near each other and occasionally nuzzle side by side. Sometimes they sun, stretching their wings wide to catch the warming rays while turning their heads to gaze at each other. They develop a bond by calling back and forth, especially when they are hunting or as they return to the nest site. These contact notes are syllables taken from the longer court-

Mountain bluebirds require territories of two to five acres to find adequate food to raise their young. (Photo copyright by Connie Toops)

ship calls. They are fairly loud and easy for the other partner to locate. In the eastern bluebird, the sound is "tur-wee" or "chee-do." Western bluebirds utter a "chweer" sound. The mountain bluebird contact call is "chur-chur."

The bond continues to strengthen as the male brings food to his mate. They also communicate with wing quivers and wing waves. These are slow, deliberate extensions of one or both wings while perched on or near the nest cavity. The sounds and visual stimuli of frequent courtship encounters solidify the pair's commitment to each other and to their impending family.

25

Top: *If a female bluebird is not satisfied with the male's first choice of nest sites, her mate may lead her on a house-hunting trip. (Eastern bluebirds, photo copyright by Connie Toops)* Above: *After bluebirds form a pair-bond, the male signals his desire to breed by bobbing and by spreading his wings. (Eastern bluebirds, photo copyright by Connie Toops)* Right: *During courtship, a male blue-bird warbles softly to his intended mate, then flies to her side and offers a morsel of food. (Mountain bluebirds, photo copyright by Jeffrey Rich)*

Bluebird Trails

A Cross-Country Sampler

Delaware County, Ohio

Delaware State Park is located on a reservoir a few miles north of Columbus. Trees grow slowly on the clay soils of the surrounding floodplain. The areas with open understory invite bluebirds. Richard Tuttle recognized that when he moved to Delaware County in the 1970s. Soon after, he began putting up nest boxes. He presently monitors 247 boxes on six trails there.

Richard's largest trail consists of 150 boxes at the state park. He normally bikes the entire route, carrying a small pack with record books, banding tools, and repair equipment. When he began the project, he used various boxes donated by the Ohio Department of Natural Resources, 4-H, and Bluebird youth groups. As the boxes aged, Tuttle replaced them with traditional front- or side-opening nest boxes. He prefers their consistency and needs only a screwdriver to open them. He attaches the boxes to metal pipes and applies a thick coat of grease to repel climbing predators. Many sites have two boxes, installed about twenty feet (6.1 m) apart. Bluebirds occupy one, with tree swallows as their neighbors.

Richard and I toured the park on a sunny May morning. The first box sheltered five young bluebirds

When banding baby bluebirds, Richard Tuttle determines their sex by the amount of blue in the wing and tail feathers. (Photo copyright by Connie Toops)

Tuttle wanted to band. He grabbed a notebook and a string of metal bands issued by the U.S. Fish and Wildlife Service. During the past quarter century, Tuttle has documented more than four thousand eastern bluebirds, nearly six thousand tree swallows, and numerous tufted titmice, Carolina chickadees, and house wrens fledging from his boxes.

Richard reached into the nest and gently removed the chicks, one by one. They snuggled quietly into a cloth bag as Tuttle pulled the nest out of the box to check it for blowfly larvae. He found very few. For a significant infestation, he would replace the nest with one fashioned from dry grass.

Richard lifted the first nestling, a male, from the bag. He recognized the sex by the amount of blue on emerging wing and tail feathers. Using special pliers, Richard closed a band around the bird's right leg. Then he returned it to the nest. He followed the same procedure for the remaining four nestlings. We left quietly, and the watchful parents returned to make certain their babies were unharmed. We banded nestlings at two more sites along the state park trail, then Richard took me a few miles into the country to see boxes with livestock guards he designed. Tuttle realized he could maximize bluebird habitat by placing nest boxes at least forty yards

In Delaware County, Ohio, Richard Tuttle has maximized bluebird habitat by placing nest boxes fitted with livestock guards in rural pastures. (Photo copyright by Connie Toops)

(36.6 m) from wren-infested fencerows in pastures with insect-laden grasses. But cattle and horses scratch themselves on traditionally mounted boxes, loosening or knocking them off. Cows also lick the grease from the posts.

Tuttle fashioned an angle-iron cross brace with barbed wire stretched in a circular pattern around the outer perimeter. The device swivels instead of providing a satisfying scratch. Cattle leave it alone. Horses sometimes run into the posts, so Tuttle adds dangling PVC pipes or flagging to warn them away. The only hazard Richard has not alleviated comes from the heavens. Two of the open-field boxes have been shattered by lightning strikes. Luckily, neither was occupied by bluebirds at the time.

Bluebirds are usually monogamous. In most cases, one male and one female share the duties of raising offspring. (Mountain bluebirds, photo copyright by Jeffrey Rich)

Betrothed or Betrayed?

After paired bluebirds select their nesting cavity, they become more secretive. The male sings less, and the female slips into the den with building materials.

Female bluebirds gather grasses, fine plant stems, or pine needles, usually within a hundred feet (30 m) of the cavity. Although males encourage their mates by being present, and occasionally with songs and wing waves or by picking up bits of nest material, they do not actively shape the egg cup. In a very unusual case in Oregon, however, a male western bluebird that lost his mate and young reacted by building a new nest.

In the semidarkness of the cavity, the female bluebird begins by poking coarse fibers into the empty spaces. As the nest takes shape, she collects finer materials with which to line the depression. She works leisurely, taking five days or so to finish. Cold, wet weather, when more time is needed to hunt for insects, slows the process.

Relatively little filler is necessary for small-floor versions of eastern bluebird houses, such as the Peterson box. Larger houses and irregular natural cavities require more insulation, and thus nest sizes vary. A bluebird nest in a fire-scarred Florida pine trunk was crammed with enough longleaf pine needles to fill a grocery bag. The average inner cup size of an eastern bluebird nest is 2½ inches (6.4 cm) across and 2 inches (5.1 cm) deep, with the lip about 3 inches (7.6 cm) below the cavity opening.

Once the nest is finished, the pair remains nearby for about five days until the female lays her first egg. Harry Power, a professor of biological sciences at Rutgers University, has studied nesting mountain bluebirds near Great Falls, Montana, for nearly two decades. Power noticed the male "escorted" or kept the female within sight in about 80 percent of her arrivals and departures at the nest during the building and brooding periods. Escorting behavior included the male's bringing nest materials to the female or flying to the entrance of the box before she departed. If the female peeked out of the box, the male seemed to signal an all-clear with a wave of his wings. He also sang or called to stay in contact with her.

Escorting safeguards the female from predators, since an attentive male can warn her of a hawk circling overhead or a snake or predatory mammal sneaking toward the nest. But this may not be the primary reason for escorting. Although bluebirds were long thought to represent the "ideal" American family by being dedicated, monogamous mates, recent research indicates this is not always so.

Bird pairing occurs in four broad categories. Monogamy, the mating of one male and female, is practiced by about 90 percent of all bird species. Swans, geese, albatrosses, and cranes are noteworthy because they remain mated for multiple seasons. Monogamy exemplifies the safety of familiarity. If birds stay together in the same territory, they will

Female bluebirds do not begin incubation until all eggs are laid. Some bluebirds exhibit such strong maternal instincts that they do not flush when nest boxes are opened by monitors. (Female western bluebird, photo copyright by Connie Toops)

know where to find food and how to defend against enemies. This low-stress lifestyle allows more energy for rearing progeny.

At the opposite extreme, promiscuous species, such as hummingbirds and grouse, have developed successful reproductive strategies that demonstrate no lasting ties between parents. After males and females mate, the females assume nesting and chick-rearing chores while males try to attract other females. In polygynous species, such as red-winged and yellow-headed blackbirds, the male breeds with a harem of females, all of whom nest within territory he defends. The rarest bonding is polyandry, which occurs in fewer than one percent of birds worldwide. Spotted sandpipers typify this behavior, in which the female is dominant and entices two males to breed within her realm. Males incubate the eggs and raise the chicks.

A term that more precisely describes the behavior of many songbirds is "apparent" monogamy. Scientists have analyzed the DNA of various songbirds to determine parentage. In many pairings thought to be monogamous, one or more of the nest mates was sired by a male other than the owner of the territory. The escorting behavior in which male bluebirds remain close to their females during nesting and brooding is designed to guard against intrusions by foreign males. By guarding the female closely, a male increases his chances of siring all or a very high percentage of the young. But when a male is away, a rival may sneak over and quickly breed with the unguarded female. The genetic advantage to any male's breeding with more than one female is that extra offspring provide more chance of the male's genes being passed to future generations.

When a male sneaks to his neighbor's nest, he leaves his mate open to mating with another male. In such cases, she is sly in her solicitations. Copulations are quick and secretive. The genetic advantage to a female is that if one suitor is infertile, another will supply viable sperm for at least some of her eggs to develop.

Some adult bluebirds do not find mates or nest sites. They are "floaters." If a floater female breeds with a resident or floater male, she will need a place to lay the egg. She will try to steal into an unguarded nest. Mated females remain close to their cavities to prevent floater females from dumping eggs. If they are to capitalize on the energy they spend on nest building, brooding, and care of young, it makes sense for residents to raise their own offspring rather than those of an unrelated female. Just as males fend off males, females chase females.

Because bluebirds seldom harass intruders of the opposite sex, males can have quick engagements with nearby females and females are open to trysts with neighboring males. A study of eastern bluebirds in South Carolina determined as many as 10 percent of the eggs under a brooding female were not hers. Up to 40 percent of the young in eastern bluebird nests may not be offspring of the male of that territory. The term applied to this unwitting care of another's young by an apparently monogamous pair is "kleptogamy."

~

The female is most fertile from three days before the first egg appears until about three days before the last egg of the clutch is laid. Bluebirds breed often in the two weeks preceding egg laying and for several days after laying begins. Sperm from the male swim through the female's cloaca and into her oviduct. More than one male can contribute sperm, and sperm remain alive within the female for several days.

Female bluebirds have only the left ovary. To reduce weight in flight, the right does not develop. As eggs are expelled into the oviduct, they are fertilized by waiting sperm. Fertilized eggs continue through the oviduct, where watery layers of albumen, shell membranes, and finally the limy shells form around each yolk. During the final few hours in the female's uterus, pigment is added to the shell.

Shell colors are by-products of metabolism. Blue and green are bile-based pigments. Brown and olive originate as blood hemoglobins. Spots and blotches on eggs of certain species are added by uterine glands shortly before the eggs are laid. The individual pattern is determined by how rapidly the egg moves and whether it twists or turns as the glands secrete pigments.

British ornithologist David Lack studied the colors of eggs from various thrushes and categorized them by the birds' nesting situations. Species using deep cavities had unmarked white eggs. Thrushes that nested in shallower holes had either white or blue eggs, some with darker speckles. Tree- or shrub-nesting thrushes had white or blue eggs with dark blotches. Ground-nesting thrushes laid eggs with brown, gray, or olive tones.

The camouflage advantage of earth-toned eggs for ground nesters is obvious. Blue eggs in shaded nests resemble the dappled patterns of sunlight and shadows, and thus are well hidden among the branches. The pale background colors of cavity-laid eggs help parents locate them in dim light.

Normal egg color for all three species of bluebirds is blue, although the paleness or richness of the color varies slightly. Proprietors of bluebird trails regularly report clutches of white eggs laid by eastern, western, and mountain bluebirds. White eggs account for roughly 5 percent of all eggs.

Amelia Laskey, who monitored nest boxes in Nashville, Tennessee, was among the first to band bluebirds and study the lineage of those laying white eggs. She determined that female eastern bluebirds hatched from white eggs could lay blue eggs and females hatched from blue eggs could lay white eggs. She traced a daughter and a granddaughter of a white-egg layer that both laid normal blue eggs. In the 1930s, Thomas Musselman documented a female hatched from a white egg that laid a clutch of white eggs in Illinois.

The laying of white eggs seems to be a trait of individual female bluebirds. There is usually no mixing of white and blue eggs in one nest. (On the rare occasion that one white egg is found among blue or vice versa, a second female probably sneaked into the cavity.) White-laying females may have a physical deformity that allows their eggs to pass through the uterus without receiving color. A Montana study determined that white mountain bluebird eggs hatched at a slightly higher rate than did blue eggs. Incidentally, partial and full albino bluebirds do occur and survive. Their feathers are weaker than those of normally pigmented birds, and their lifespans may be short. Albinos do not necessarily hatch from or lay white eggs.

~

Female bluebirds lay one egg each morning in quiet

Top inset: *Male bluebirds "escort" their mates during courtship and the early stages of nesting so rivals will not breed with the paired female. (Mountain bluebirds, photo copyright by Connie Toops) Center inset: About 5 percent of all clutches of bluebird eggs lack the typical light blue color. (Photo copyright by Connie Toops)*

visits to the nest. The oval eggs of eastern and western bluebirds are approximately .82 inch by .63 inch (2.1 cm x 1.6 cm), roughly the size of a table grape. Mountain bluebird eggs are incrementally larger. All have a glossy luster. Yearling eastern bluebirds routinely produce four eggs in their first clutch and three in the second. Older females average five eggs in the first nest of the season and four in the second clutch. The third clutch, if laid, may contain three or four eggs. A few instances of eastern bluebirds with seven eggs in one nest are known, though some of these may have been cases of kleptogamy.

Western bluebirds, although the same size as eastern, average one more egg than eastern bluebirds in each nesting situation. That is, yearling western bluebirds lay five eggs, then four in the second nest. Older females average six eggs in the first nest and five thereafter. Numerous sets of seven eggs have been reported. Mountain bluebirds, which are slightly more robust, have larger clutches. Yearling females lay five or six eggs, while older females may lay eight. Several mountain bluebird nests containing ten eggs have been discovered.

Normally, female bluebirds begin to incubate after the final egg of the set is deposited. Sometimes a female bluebird will begin a day early or wait several days before starting. If the eggs freeze in her absence, they will crack and spoil. If they cool to near freezing, the mucous layer beneath the shell thickens into a gluey substance that eventually makes it hard for the hatchling to peck through. If temperatures inside the cavity remain at 50 to 65 degrees Fahrenheit (10°–18° C), the eggs stay fertile but do not develop until the female begins to brood. Unseasonably warm weather can speed embryo development without brooding. In this case, the first egg will hatch a day ahead of schedule.

Most songbirds do not incubate until all eggs are laid. This ensures babies arrive at the same time and compete equally for food. Barn owls and other birds of prey incubate beginning with the first egg. Their babies stairstep in age. While all survive in years of abundant prey, only the strongest persist when food is scarce. The strategy of even-aged young employed by bluebirds succeeds because the insects they feed upon are usually plentiful enough for all nestlings to eat their fill.

Bottom inset: *Although western bluebirds are the same size as eastern, female western bluebirds lay more eggs. Sets of four to six eggs are normal, but clutches of seven western bluebird eggs are sometimes reported. (Photo copyright by Connie Toops) Above: Male bluebirds gather a few pine needles or bits of grass in their courtship displays, but females construct the nests. (Female eastern bluebird, photo copyright by Paul Zimmerman)*

Bluebird Trails

A Cross-Country Sampler

Rockford, Ohio

With terrain as flat as a billiard table and rich glacial soils, west-central Ohio is a farmer's dream. I drove past fields of wheat, robust shoots of corn emerging from the black earth, and green pastures with dairy cattle grazing. But the only birds I saw were starlings, house sparrows, and house finches. Then, as I crossed from Van Wert to Mercer County, I spotted a male bluebird on a utility wire. Across the road was a trim green house with a nest box on the front lawn, bluebirds on the mailbox, and a decorative wooden bluebird by the shop door. I knew I had found Robert and Lois Rager. They welcomed me into a home as warm and cozy as the inside of a bluebird's nest.

In 1985, eastern bluebirds took up residence in the Rager's martin house. These were the first bluebirds Bob and Lois had seen in years. The next year, Bob added bluebird houses to his yard and gave some to neighbors. Sparrows claimed most of them, but bluebirds nested too, and the news made the local paper. An area North American Bluebird Society member called the Ragers. That started Bob thinking about a bluebird trail.

Neighboring farms average a hundred acres (40 hectares), with boundaries marked by sturdy cement corner posts. There are grassy strips ideal for bluebird foraging along the rural roads and around farmsteads. Rager knew many of his neighbors and now had an excuse to meet others who had likely spots for the birds. Since his name and phone number are stenciled on each box, Rager also receives requests for them. His trail now in-

Robert Rager monitors a trail of 130 bluebird nest boxes on the fertile farmlands of northwestern Ohio. (Photo copyright by Connie Toops)

cludes 130 boxes. At age seventy-five, he rides a moped on the sixty miles (97 km) of roads that cover this grid, checking a few boxes every day during the nesting season.

Bob offered to show me part of the trail, so we headed east from his house along a country road. "The farmer takes good care of that box," Rager commented as we looked across a cornfield to a neat house and barn surrounded by shade trees. "He always has bluebirds."

"This one has a bluebird with five eggs," Bob nodded as he navigated his station wagon down the road, "and that one has tree swallows." A female swallow's head peeked from the box as she surveyed a herd of Holsteins in the adjacent pasture. Rager pulled onto the narrow shoulder of the road and walked to a box mounted on a cement post. His large hands lifted the door as he spoke quietly to the bird inside. "Look here," he whispered, pointing to a female bluebird on the nest. "Sometimes she'll step aside and let me count the eggs. Then I close up the box."

We stopped next at a small cemetery. "Cemeteries should be good places for bluebirds," Rager stated as he cleaned a nest box, "but I've had trouble with sparrows." Farther down the road we approached a woodlot. "We always have bluebirds here," Bob bragged, pointing to a box on the fence. "These should be ready to fly in a few days."

A male house sparrow departed as we stopped the car. Rager opened the box, and his smile faded. One dead fledgling bluebird remained inside. Another lay on the ground. "Four days ago this box had five healthy bluebirds in it," Rager mused. "I'll be back with a trap."

We passed some apple trees. "I had an interesting situation here," Rager recalled. "The county widened the road and one of the workers moved the box out of the way—propped it up post and all between some concrete blocks. There was a bluebird on a nest inside, so I came out and put up a new pole, then transferred the box. All of the babies fledged."

We stopped for Rager to look at box 58. He grinned as he returned. "I've taken sparrows out of that box four times this year," he reported. "Now there's a bluebird nest with one egg."

In a grandfatherly way, Rager knew the status of every box on his trail. Lois confided they leave Florida each winter to be home for the arrival of the first bluebird. "The bluebirds give him energy and enthusiasm," she observed. She proudly told me Bob has inspired thirty or forty others to tend bluebird boxes.

Later, I received a note, penned the day after my visit. "Remember box 55 with the dead bluebird?" Bob wrote. "I went back in the PM and set a trap. The male sparrow paid the price."

The Marvel of New Life

Hormonal changes occur near the end of a female bluebird's egg-laying cycle. Her belly skin reddens because of an increased blood supply. Downy breast feathers fall out. She presses the resulting area of warm skin, called the brood patch, against her eggs. Direct contact with the female, whose internal temperature is 106 degrees Fahrenheit (41° C), keeps the eggs an extra 10 degrees Fahrenheit (5.6° C) warmer than if she did not have a brood patch.

Although the male brings food to the nest, the female leaves now and then to forage, drink, and bathe. The male does not form a brood patch and thus cannot brood, but in her absence he may sit on the eggs to conserve some of their warmth. The female seems to sense how long she can stay away. She remains on the nest more in cold or wet weather than on mild days. Ben Pinkowski's research on eastern bluebird nests in Michigan indicates that the female can leave eggs for nearly a day during the first week of incubation without damaging the embryos. During the second week, she cannot be absent more than a few hours or the embryos will chill too much. The female sleeps on the nest while brooding and for the first week after the babies hatch. As nestlings mature, both parents roost nearby.

Hot temperatures are as dangerous to the eggs as cold. Heat swelters in poorly insulated boxes on sunny summer days. Normal brooding temperatures range from 95 to 98 degrees Fahrenheit (35°–36.7° C). Blue-bird eggs addle at 107 degrees (41.7° C), and temperatures in thin-walled boxes can easily exceed this.

Eastern bluebirds usually require thirteen or fourteen days to hatch. Western and mountain bluebird babies normally hatch in fourteen days. During periods of inclement weather, which slows embryo development, females of all three species have incubated for nearly three weeks before the chicks hatched.

Baby bluebirds enter the world after pecking around the middle of their shells with an egg tooth, a hard tip on the beak that subsequently falls off. The naked, wet hatchling is usually exhausted from the several hours' work it takes to break free. But mother is quite attentive. She eats some of the shell, recycling the calcium. She passes the remainder to her mate or flies off with it, dropping pieces far enough from the nest to avoid attracting ants or predators.

The babies are born with only a wisp of down on their heads and backs, so they cannot stay warm on their own. Baby robins and thrushes have much more down when they hatch, yet young bluebirds enjoy a higher survival rate. They benefit because the cavity affords more protection from the weather and predators than an open nest does. The female broods diligently while the male brings small bits of soft insect food for the babies. He also feeds his mate. Incubating females often sit tight when nest boxes are opened by human monitors. A bird's instinctive reaction is to flee from threats, so this devotion to the hatchlings

Female bluebirds incubate the eggs and brood tiny chicks with few interruptions. As the babies mature, females join their mates in hunting food for the growing family. (Female mountain bluebird, photo copyright by Steve and Dave Maslowski)

is remarkable.

When they hatch, baby bluebirds weigh an ounce (28 g), the same as a first-class letter. They are the size of the end of a human thumb, with naked, salmon-colored skin. Their heads seem grotesquely large, and eyes are not yet developed. They have naked nubbins for wings and weak, spindly legs. Bellies swell with remains of the egg yolk.

These homely little creatures spend most of their time huddled beneath mother's warm breast, asleep. The male brings food often enough to feed each nestling at least twice an hour. When a parent arrives at the box and gives its characteristic greeting call, the nestlings instinctively gape. They stretch their wobbly necks and open their mouths wide. In the dim light of the cavity, their orange throat lining presents an easy target for parents. Adults are stimulated to feed by the abrupt peeping sounds uttered by the babies.

After young bluebirds eat, they expel excrement encased in thin membranes. During the first few days, baby bluebirds' digestive tracts are not fully developed, so nutrition remains in the food that passes through them. Adults sometimes eat the droppings. As babies mature, adults collect and remove the fecal sacs. They randomly drop as many as sixty to seventy of these little bundles per day in an effort to keep the nest clean and free of scent.

By day three, baby bluebirds weigh two ounces (56 g) and have soft gray down along the edges of the wings, head, and spine. The skin beneath these areas appears blue-black. It is colored by developing feathers that will pop through in the second week.

Weather plays an important role in chick development. Adult bluebirds survive cold, wet, or snowy periods when insects are dormant by eating fruits. But without a high-protein diet, nestlings weaken. If females sense their mates are not bringing sufficient invertebrate food for the youngsters, they join the hunt. When left too long in the cold, babies chill so much they cannot lift their heads to eat when parents return. If they are not brooded immediately, they may die.

Earl Gillis tabulated many years of weather records for Oregon's northern Willamette Valley. He correlated them with the success of western bluebirds on a trail southwest of Portland. When daily temperatures fall below an average of 52 degrees Fahrenheit (11° C), especially when accompanied by periods of rainy weather, insects go into hiding. Bluebirds with young in the nest are at risk. Harry Power noticed mountain bluebird nesting success was very high in central Montana during hot, dry years in the mid-1980s. Insects such as grasshoppers, crickets, and caterpillars were abundant, active, and easy for bluebirds to spot among the sparse grasses.

The nestlings' eyes open by day eight. They weigh six to seven ounces (168–196 g) and are covered with emerging feathers. The babies are well enough insulated by now that mother can help her mate hunt. Parents bring an array of beetles, grasshoppers, crickets, and cutworms to the youngsters, averaging one visit every five minutes. Mulberries, blackberries, and wild cherries ripen in time to be fed to chicks of second and third broods. These fruits may provide essential moisture on hot summer days.

Nestlings recognize their parents first by sound, then by sight. The hungry babies respond to their parents by cheeping. The hungriest call loudest and gape intently. Recently fed birds are quiet. This ensures that babies eat in rotation. Persistent calls also attract predators. When danger is near, parents give abrupt "chuck" or "upp" calls. The nestlings cower silently until danger passes.

By day eleven, the little birds preen themselves, picking at the sheaths of their emerging feathers. They instinctively reach to a gland at the base of the tail, rub oil on their beaks, and spread it to condition the feathers. They stretch and hop about within the cavity, strengthening leg and wing muscles. When they are two weeks old, babies are agile enough to cling near the entrance and peer out, watching their parents and any other creatures in the vicinity. By now they have a narrow ring of white feathers around each eye and speckled gray breasts.

❧

Eastern bluebird babies are nestbound an average of

Opposite: *Baby bluebirds are usually exhausted by the effort of breaking free from their shell. Born with only a wisp of down on their heads and backs, they must snuggle beneath mother's breast for more than a week to stay warm until their feathers appear. (Mountain bluebird nest, photo copyright by Connie Toops) Opposite inset: Parents feed each nestling about twice an hour. The babies gape to expose orange throat linings, which in the dim light of the cavity are bright targets for parents to deposit food. (Nest of eastern bluebirds, photo copyright by Michael L. Smith)*

eighteen days. If food is readily available, they may fledge a day or two earlier. Western and mountain bluebirds remain in their nests twenty or twenty-one days. Mountain bluebirds facing adverse weather have remained in nests as long as twenty-three days. By the time fledglings leave, they weigh slightly more than their parents.

Parents feed and care for babies most efficiently if they fledge together. Adults coax youngsters by calling while bobbing from perch to perch with food in their beaks. They stay within view, but out of reach. A hungry chick peers from the nest. Its parent hovers inches from the entrance, luring the baby with a tasty morsel. Finally, a tentative jump and a surprised flutter launch the fluffball into the air. It aims for the nearest perch. Flight is instinctive, but landings need to be practiced a few times before they are graceful.

Parents reward the brave fledgling with food, then lure a sibling. The scene is repeated several times as babies empty from the box. For a few days after leaving the nest, youngsters remain close to each other. They huddle shoulder to shoulder for warmth and companionship, especially at night or during storms. They hide from hawks, jays, or magpies in tree branches or among grasses and forbs. They plead for food using repetitive peeps, audible a quarter mile (0.4 km) away.

Baby bluebirds know how to beg, preen, and fly. They must learn to sing, hunt, bathe, and avoid enemies. Even though they will not sing until the following year, they need to hear adults give courting calls before they mature in order to mimic these notes and phrases next year.

As they watch their parents perching on low limbs, power lines, or fences, they gradually realize adults are seeing prey on the ground and flying down to capture it. Mountain bluebirds, which live in areas without many perches, have perfected a hovering technique in which they flutter a few feet above the ground and then drop on prey. In comparison to eastern or western bluebirds, the wings and tails of mountain bluebirds are longer and their wingbeats are slower.

Bluebirds can discern barely moving green caterpillars on blades of similarly colored grass from distances of up to seventy-five feet (23 m). Peter Gold-

man tallied the hunting success of eastern bluebirds and noted that adults caught prey on two of every three attempts. Juveniles caught prey one of every three tries. Adults perch longer between attempts. Goldman theorized that youngsters do not have the experience to reject possible prey items at a distance, and thus fly to investigate more often.

Although introduced by their parents to a wide range of invertebrate foods, including maggots, cutworms, caterpillars, various hard-shelled beetles, katydids, crickets, grasshoppers, butterflies, dragonflies, spiders, centipedes, and millipedes, young bluebirds learn by positive reinforcement of their own successful catches what foods are easy to handle and taste best. Bright yellow and black monarch caterpillars, for instance, are easy to see and capture. But one taste of their flesh, made bitter by the milkweed sap they consume, is enough to make a young bluebird spit out its mouthful and never make the mistake again. Bluebirds have occasionally been seen eating small frogs and snails. The rarity of such events suggests these are harder to find or less tasty than their main diet of arthropods.

Besides the normal drop-hunting technique, one in ten feeding attempts for eastern and western bluebirds and three in ten attempts for mountain bluebirds succeed in plucking an insect from the air. Occasionally bluebirds hover near trees, picking food from the leaves. When a bluebird lands to catch prey, it may remain on the ground to eat. More often, it returns to a perch before dining. Grasshoppers and similar hard-shelled creatures are beaten against the perch to break the chitinous shell. After eating, bluebirds clean and hone their bills by scraping them back and forth on a hard surface.

For the first week after fledglings leave the nest, they remain hidden and parents supply their food. If the season is long enough, parental courtship activities resume. The female attends to the nest. The male continues to guard and feed the babies. By this time, they follow him and beg aggressively. Two weeks after fledging, youngsters begin hunting on their own. Another week or two of practice makes them self-sufficient.

❦

Summer courtships are not lengthy. Mated pairs often remain together, with the female building a new nest and laying another clutch of eggs in several days' less time than in the spring. If one of the pair has disappeared, an unmated floater may become the new partner.

The initiation dates of second and third broods are less predictable than those of first nests. Competitors may evict bluebirds, predators may consume eggs or young in midcycle, or vagaries of weather may delay nesting. From years of records for eastern bluebirds in central Ohio, Richard Tuttle determined that first eggs are laid about April 1. Those birds fledge the first week of May. Second broods begin during the last week of May and fledge near the end of June. Third clutches, if they occur, are laid after July 12.

Southern initiation dates begin about three weeks earlier. The longer breeding season makes third broods more common in the South. On rare occasions, four clutches have been reported. In northern states and southern Canada, nesting occurs two weeks later than in Ohio. In Tuttle's study area, only 5 percent of the clutches are laid after mid-July. Elsie Eltzroth has tallied western bluebird nesting success near Corvallis, Oregon, since 1977. She believes fewer than 10 percent of these birds attempt a third brood. Third clutches seldom occur in northern areas. Many bluebirds with young in nests during July and early August are raising a second brood that was delayed by predation, competition, or inexperience.

Although a high percentage of bluebirds do raise second broods, Bluebird Recovery Program records from the Midwest show fledging success drops from between 75 to 95 percent in the first clutch to about 55 percent in the second.

❧

Spring is a delightful time for bird-lovers. Territorial songs of dozens of species fill the air. Everywhere an attentive birder looks, there are signs of reproduction—birds carrying bits of nest material, nests hidden among the blooming shrubs, parents with food in their beaks. During late spring and summer, bird populations swell to their maximum numbers of the year.

The longer babies are confined to the nest, however, the more chances increase that sounds, smells, or the sight of parents making repeated trips will alert predators of their location. Just as spring is a time of blossoming and reproduction, summer begins the reign of predators. Cats slink from shrub to shrub, jays lurk in the branches above, and snakes harvest a bounty of eggs and chicks wherever they can climb. Larry Zeleny, who maintained a bluebird trail in Beltsville, Maryland, for nearly three decades, commented, "The most dangerous day in the life of a bluebird is the day it fledges."

How long do bluebirds live? Unlike humans, most bluebirds die within their first year. Inexperienced fledglings are prime targets for predators. They also die in accidents such as hitting windows or radio towers. They may not find enough food or adequate shelter from winter weather.

A study of the closely related European robin revealed that one of every ten fledglings reached adulthood. After adulthood, about 50 percent of the population died annually. For example, if 50,000 European robins fledged during the summer of 1995, only 5,000 would survive to mate and breed in 1996. Of these, 2,500 would live to their second adult summer; 1,250 would survive to the third year; 625 would remain in the fourth year, and so on. By 2005, their tenth year, only ten of the original European robins would still be alive.

Like their European relatives, bluebirds that survive the first year have a fairly constant mortality rate thereafter. The "average" bluebird is about two years old, but a few individuals live much longer. So far, the oldest eastern, western, and mountain bluebirds known from band recoveries have all been seven years old.

Top inset: *If cold, rainy weather forces insects into hiding, male bluebirds may not find enough for their babies to eat. Females will temporarily abandon their brooding chores to join the hunt, but if they stay away too long, nestlings may die. (Female western blue-bird, photo copyright by Connie Toops)*

Center inset: At about two weeks of age, baby bluebirds begin to peer out of the cavity, waiting for their parents to arrive with food. (Eastern bluebirds, photo copyright by Michael L. Smith) Bottom inset: Bluebirds can see small insects at distances of seventy-five feet (23 m) or more. They often perch on a dead branch or exposed wire, then drop to the ground to grab their prey. (Male mountain bluebird, photo copyright by Connie Toops) Above: Once they leave the nest, young bluebirds remain hidden while their parents bring them food. (Male western bluebird with fledgling, photo copyright by Connie Toops)

Stillwater, Minnesota

Dark green pines and spruces cloaked the rolling hills of the St. Croix Valley. Not far past a deep, cool lake that hosted a family of loons, I turned at another driveway with a painted wooden bluebird displayed prominently near the door to the shop. I was now in eastern Minnesota, visiting Dave Ahlgren, who has fashioned more Peterson bluebird houses than anyone else. Dave's wife Jan led me to the screened porch so we could watch a pair of bluebirds nesting in the backyard as we talked.

Dave is an airline pilot who enjoys wildlife. He is also handy with wood. Ten years ago Carrol Henderson, supervisor of the Minnesota Department of Natural Resources (DNR) Nongame Wildlife Program, was compiling plans for various nest boxes. He asked Dave to construct a sample of each to check the dimensions. Dave discovered some errors, which were corrected before the DNR published its popular *Woodworking for Wildlife*. Henderson also planned several bluebird workshops and wanted a Peterson nest box for each of the five hundred participants. Dave agreed to construct them. When his name was listed on a workshop resource list, Ahlgren began to receive a steady stream of orders for Peterson boxes.

"This is actually a big hobby," Dave said. "Word of mouth is the only advertising we've ever had. Yet this has continued to grow until the business is totally out of hand," he joked. "I've probably made about thirty thousand boxes by now. In February, March, and April, I frequently work sixteen hours a day."

Airline pilot Dave Ahlgren donates much of his spare time making Peterson nest boxes. (Photo copyright by Connie Toops)

"Peterson boxes have small parts and weird angles," Dave explained. "It is one of the more difficult box plans to follow, but it's important that it be constructed to Peterson specifications. I prefer to ship them out as kits, but I do put some of them together," he continued. Dave donates his time, charging only for materials and shipping. He chooses western red cedar for the fronts, backs, and tops of the boxes and primed hardboard for the sides. He cuts and drills pieces in multiples to speed the process.

Dave and Jan tend nest boxes around their house. Jan keeps two feeding trays stocked with mealworms, which she buys by the thousand, so visitors can see the birds up close. Both are active promoters of the Bluebird Recovery Program, and Jan spends hours on the phone answering bluebird questions.

"Why do we live and breathe bluebirds?" she mused, pondering my question. "Well, because we learn of people—as many as two or three a week—that don't know about bluebirds or haven't seen them. Many of them come here, and they see their first, or the first in a long time, and they are thrilled. We meet good people, and it's fun to share with others, so I guess that's why we still do this."

Dave and Jan Ahlgren have helped many individuals see their first bluebirds and have rekindled interest among people who have not seen the birds for decades. (Photo copyright by Connie Toops)

Above: At Finley National Wildlife Refuge in Oregon, I observed adult western bluebirds catching food for their nestlings. (Male western bluebird, photo copyright by Connie Toops) Left: As adults made regular feeding trips to the nest box, a curious youngster from an earlier brood watched its parents. Then the eight-week-old fledgling began bringing insects to feed its younger siblings. (Western bluebirds, photo copyright by Connie Toops)

Family Ties

For bluebirds, care of second and third broods is similar to care of the first, with one major exception. Youngsters from earlier broods may help raise their new siblings.

I watched this firsthand at Finley National Wildlife Refuge, in Oregon's Willamette Valley, where I photographed a nest box on a pasture fence. As I put up my blind, which resembles a camouflaged pup tent, I heard adult western bluebirds calling to one another in slightly worried tones from the oak trees behind me. Once I disappeared inside, they were satisfied that danger had passed.

Soon after, the male landed on the fence with a fat, white grub in his beak. Clamorous chirping greeted his arrival. He popped into the box and departed a few moments later, carrying a fecal sac. The female waited on a post with a grasshopper in her beak. She, too, fed the nestlings and departed with a fecal sac.

I photographed both parents at the box several times before I realized a fledgling was sitting quietly on the barbed wire fence, several feet to the right. Through my telephoto lens, I saw its narrow white eye ring and the dappled pattern of gray and white on its breast.

The fledgling watched quizzically as adults carried food to the box and disappeared inside. Once the male landed near the youngster with an insect in its beak, but the fledgling did not beg. About five minutes later, the young bird cocked its head and stared intently into the sparse grasses. It dropped to the ground about fifteen feet (4.6 m) in front of its perch and picked up a small insect. Instead of gobbling this tidbit, it flew back to the fence and sat looking at the nest box.

The young bird shuffled closer to the box and looked in all directions. After several minutes, still holding the insect in its beak, it flew to the roof of the nest box. Uncertainly, it leaned over the roof and peeked into the hole. The male arrived with another grasshopper. He entered the box and fed the chirping babies. The fledgling watched intently. When the male departed, the youngster flew to the entrance. It looked inside, leaned back to scan the sky, then peered in the box again. After several moments of indecision, the young bird finally tipped its head into the box. When it backed away, the insect was gone.

About ten minutes later, the fledgling western bluebird returned with a winged insect in its beak. Less hesitantly, it flew to the box, leaned in, and emerged without the insect. Its confident manner convinced me that I had previously witnessed one of the bird's first attempts to feed its siblings.

While watching the fledgling, I noticed a silver U.S. Fish and Wildlife Service band on its right leg and a narrow, red plastic band on its left leg. Researcher Elsie Eltzroth had marked the nestling on May 20, 1993, at age fourteen days. It left the nest a week later. I photographed the bird on July 14, fifty-five days after it hatched. In that short time, this

Helping behavior is not unusual among bluebirds. Juveniles from earlier broods may assist in feeding siblings of a second or third clutch. When an adult dies, relatives or neighbors often join in caring for the babies. (Western bluebirds, photo copyright by Connie Toops)

western bluebird had learned to feed itself and was also sharing food with younger siblings. In Minnesota, Dick Peterson documented a captive, orphaned eastern bluebird that at thirty-three days of age fed a fifteen-day-old orphan. The precise time that fledglings stop begging and begin helping varies from nest to nest, but it is not uncommon for birds only two or three months old to assist their parents.

Bluebirds are not unique in having family members help with chick-raising chores. This behavior has been documented in more than a hundred species of birds worldwide. It is common in the raven family. Unmated crows and scrub jays up to four years old remain with the family as helpers. They defend the site, feed nestlings, and sometimes brood eggs or young. Their reward is that when parents die, experienced offspring inherit the territory as their own breeding space.

In eastern, western, and mountain bluebirds, helpers range from recently fledged juveniles to birds a year or more old. Larry Zeleny watched an eastern bluebird nest in which the female died when babies

of her second brood were seven days old. Two eight-week-old males from the first brood joined their father in successfully raising the nestlings. Zeleny documented another nest in which the adult male disappeared, but an adult female and a female sibling from an earlier brood joined the widow to raise her young.

Similarly, when a nest of eight-day-old western bluebirds near Newberg, Oregon, lost the female, a neighboring male assisted the father in raising the nestlings. With the female absent, monitors placed a hand-warmer in the box to keep the four nestlings warm until they were about twelve days old and well feathered. While male birds will feed the babies, they cannot brood them. The father and the assistant, both banded, were believed to be siblings from the previous year.

In Michigan, Ben Pinkowski observed banded eastern bluebirds that nested in the same box two successive years. One of the male offspring from the first year sired a family of his own nearby in the second year. When the son's fledglings were old enough, he brought them to the box still in use by his parents. The parents, joined by fledglings from their first brood of the year and last season's son, fed their second brood. Pinkowski tallied the feeding visits as: father, 34 percent; son, 28 percent; mother, 27 percent; fledglings from the first brood, 10 percent. All five nestlings fledged, which was the greatest number of young the parents ever raised at one time.

The frequency with which relatives help at the nest suggests that bluebirds recognize family ties. Helpers enable parents to raise more birds, while the apprentices learn skills they will need to become good parents. They also benefit by remaining in the protected surroundings of their own family group. In colonial-nesting gulls, a young bird that wanders from its nest is often pecked to death by other adults if it blunders into their territory. If a fledgling bluebird wanders into another pair's territory, it is more likely to be fed than chased away.

❧

Bluebird families remain together during the late summer and fall. As daylight fades, hormonal changes regulate the onset of the annual molt cycle. Bluebirds' worn feathers are gradually shed and replaced by new ones. Feathers account for a tenth of a bluebird's weight, so it takes a significant amount of protein-based energy to replace them. The molt period occurs after the energy needs of courtship, nesting, and raising young have been met, but before cold weather wipes out summer's abundance of insects. In order to replenish feathers, bluebirds eat heartily during the molt period. They also spend quite a bit of time bathing and grooming.

Although many birds molt twice annually, bluebirds renew a complete set of feathers only once a year. The wing and tail feathers grown by nestlings are retained throughout their first year. By autumn, their dappled juvenile body plumage is replaced with the brighter colors of adulthood.

At the end of the molt period, fresh plumage shows finer details, such as a buffy tint on breast feathers and pale white edging on wing feathers of female mountain bluebirds. Most, but not all, male western bluebirds have rufous edges on their back feathers in fresh fall plumage. As time passes, the edges wear. Older feathers are more uniformly blue.

Bluebirds stray from their nesting territories in search of food during the molting period. Mountain bluebirds often wander to higher elevations. But bluebird families usually return to their nest sites in the fall. Parents and offspring from one or several broods gather, calling to each other in soft voices while taking turns investigating the cavity inside and out. Sometimes one or more of the birds will carry a few pieces of grass or pine needles into the box, as though reinforcing the idea that this is a place to nest. These gatherings are repeated over several weeks in autumn.

J. D. Brawn studied a group of sixty western bluebird nest boxes in ponderosa pines near Flagstaff, Arizona. Late in the summer he observed juveniles of both sexes (more males than females) sitting on or near unoccupied nest boxes. When unrelated adult or immature bluebirds approached, these birds defended the area with short bursts of aggressive flight. Once interlopers were repelled, defenders returned to their posts. The following year, Brawn noted 43 percent of the users of these nest sites had defended them the previous year.

Ben Pinkowski followed an extended family of color-banded eastern bluebirds in southeastern Michigan throughout the year. In early fall, the five offspring investigated their natal box with their parents. Most of the young migrated south in late September, traveling with a small flock of bluebirds from the area. Interestingly, the parents and a male offspring remained in the nesting territory for the winter. By late March the following year, the parents started to renest at their former box. In early April, the overwintering yearling male attracted a mate. That pair set up housekeeping within a mile (1.6 km) of his birthplace.

❧

The Indian summer days of autumn are often referred to as "bluebird weather" by old-timers. As cooler temperatures forced insects into hiding, flocks of a hundred or more bluebirds would gather and drift southward. Point Pelee, a peninsula on the north shore of Lake Erie, is a natural gathering place for migrants. Percy Taverner and Bradshaw Swales wrote of an eastern bluebird sighting there in late October 1905, "They were in flocks almost as dense as blackbirds. . . . When they lit and were viewed from a little distance, they were in sufficient numbers to give the

Bluebirds sometimes return to their nest sites in autumn. These fall visits may help establish ownership of the territory for the following year. (Western bluebirds, photo copyright by Hugh P. Smith, Jr.)

whole bush a decidedly blueish cast."

Many eastern bluebirds that reside north of 40 degrees north latitude migrate south for the winter. Eastern bluebirds banded in the Northeast have been spotted in the Carolinas, Georgia, and Florida. Bluebirds banded in Wisconsin have been found overwintering in Missouri, Arkansas, and Tennessee. Marked eastern bluebirds from Minnesota have been discovered in Alabama, Louisiana, and Texas in the winter. Birds that summer in the northwestern part of the range move south to Nebraska, Oklahoma, and Texas. But some individuals have remained as far north as Vermont, Ontario, Michigan, and Minnesota for the winter. In coastal Massachusetts, a few bluebirds overwinter by feeding on bayberries and seeking shelter in red cedar trees.

Western bluebirds leave higher summer elevations for nearby valleys or coastal areas, where temperatures remain warm enough for insect activity throughout the winter. Some western bluebirds migrate south from their summering areas. Two males banded in north-central Washington were discovered in Corvallis, Oregon, in late winter.

Snowstorms push mountain bluebirds from northern habitats to the southwestern United States. Migrants follow river valleys and canyons. Some travel south to central Mexico. Mountain bluebirds banded in Manitoba have wintered in Texas and Oklahoma. Birds banded in western Canada have overwintered in New Mexico, where flocks of several hundred gather in stands of piñon pine. In southern portions of their range, resident mountain bluebirds descend to lower elevations for the winter.

Since mountain bluebirds are found from Alaska to Mexico and travel longer distances in migration than do eastern or western bluebirds, they have more chance of being blown off course. In the past several decades, individual mountain bluebirds have been recorded in Wisconsin, Minnesota, Iowa, Michigan, Illinois, Pennsylvania, Kentucky, Mississippi, North Carolina, and north to Point Barrow, Alaska.

Unlike most songbirds, robins and bluebirds migrate by day rather than at night. When bluebirds were abundant, hunters and farmers harvesting crops noticed their fall passage by the lisping contact calls the birds uttered in flight. Ornithologist Frank

Chapman wrote, "So associated is [the bluebird's] voice with the birth and death of the seasons that to me his song is freighted with all the gladness of springtime, while the sad notes of the birds passing southward tell me more plainly than the falling leaves that the year is dying."

In migrant flocks and on their wintering grounds, it is not unusual to see other songbirds with bluebirds. Eastern bluebirds are joined by palm, pine, and yellow-rumped warblers. Western and mountain bluebirds often feed among robins and cedar waxwings. House finches associate with all three species.

A quarter of the birds that summer in North America go elsewhere in the winter. Instead of staying in a well-known place, coping with cold and possible food shortages, they chance the hazards of long-distance travel to a warmer place where food should be more abundant. In the new location, however, birds must fight for feeding rights. They may also need to recognize new species of plant or insect foods.

Bluebirds that linger in the north face shorter days in which to gather food and long, cold nights. They conserve nearly half the energy required to sleep on an exposed branch by snoozing in protected roosts, such as tree cavities or nest boxes. On cold winter nights, clusters of two to four birds may roost together. Communal roosting is most common in late winter. Up to two dozen bluebirds will snuggle in bitterly cold weather, with tails inward and heads facing the cavity walls. They tuck their beaks into their downy feathers, breathing warm air trapped against their bodies, and pull their feet up to their bellies so minimal flesh is exposed. In a similar group of black-tailed gnatcatchers, the inner cavity temperature was 53 degrees Fahrenheit (29.4° C) warmer than the outside air.

Bluebirds require extra calories to stay warm in the winter. Although insects provide protein for growth, the sugars in berries convert more quickly into heat energy. Bluebirds eat copious quantities of winter fruits, including dogwood, wild grape, mountain ash, hackberry, sumac, and holly. Western bluebirds relish mistletoe. They will travel upslope from nesting territories to glean the ripening fruits before severe winter storms set in.

Bluebirds live "on the edge" in winter, moving south until they discover enough fruits, with occa-sional arthropods on warm days, to sustain them. In most years, they gamble correctly, investing less energy in hazardous migration and weathering short cold spells in sheltered roosts. When it is very cold, however, they cannot exist long without food or their meager fat reserves will be exhausted.

In tests of survival capabilities, house sparrows endured without food for sixty-seven hours at 85 degrees Fahrenheit (29.4° C). When temperatures dropped to 5 degrees Fahrenheit (-15° C), they could go without food for only fifteen hours. At -30 degrees (-34.4° C), sparrows needed food within seven hours or they succumbed to the cold.

David Pitts studied wintering eastern bluebirds in northwestern Tennessee. Bluebirds from the north-central states migrate to this region. Resident bluebirds either stay near summer territories or move short distances to better winter habitat. The area normally experiences mild weather interspersed with brief cold spells. Every few years, harsh winter storms catch bluebirds without adequate food and shelter. During the winter of 1960–61, daily temperatures averaged 7 degrees Fahrenheit (3.8° C) below normal. The coldest temperature was -4 degrees Fahrenheit (-20° C). Forty-four percent of the bluebirds in Pitts's study area died during the cold spell.

The winter of 1976–77 was again remarkable, with only fifteen days in January above freezing in the study area. Snow covered the ground most of the month, with January temperatures 15 degrees Fahrenheit (8.3° C) colder than normal. Insects were sluggish and berries often were ice-covered. Droppings in roost boxes indicated that the bluebirds ate many sumac berries, which were abundant. But with large, indigestible seeds, they are not very nutritious. Pitts recovered nineteen dead bluebirds from roost boxes. They were 26 percent lighter than normal. Instead of death by suffocation, as might be theorized for a bird on the bottom of a dozen others in a box, Pitts believed these birds were so weakened by food shortage that very cold nights depleted their energy reserves.

Twenty-five pairs of bluebirds inhabited Pitts's study area in the summer of 1976. Only fourteen pairs were observed in 1977. Many of the adults and young were banded in 1976. None of the nesting females in 1977 carried bands. Pitts theorized that most of the birds present in 1977 moved into the region after the winter storms had passed.

Harsh winters cause short-term declines in bluebird populations. The winters of 1894–95, 1905–06, 1911–12, 1939–40, and 1950–51 were marked by icy weather in the southern states. Eastern bluebird populations dropped sharply after each. But bluebirds are capable of reproducing prolifically when they have good nest sites and mild spring weather so there is abundant food for chicks.

This was not the case in 1958. Bluebird populations were declining, for several reasons, from their turn-of-the-century abundance. This harsh winter killed many of the remaining eastern bluebirds. Another cold winter in 1961 kept their numbers very low. By then, introduced starlings had chased bluebirds from nest cavities and also had invaded bluebird wintering habitat in large flocks. Starlings systematically strip fruits that bluebirds rely upon for winter food, making it all the harder to survive stressful periods of cold, icy weather.

The winter of 1992–93 was marked by very cold temperatures in February and March in the East and the Great Lakes states, along with a mid-March blizzard that killed numerous resident and migrant eastern bluebirds in the South and along the East Coast. That spring and summer were cool and damp from the Northeast through the Midwest to the West Coast. Nest box surveys revealed lower-than-normal reproduction for all three bluebird species during 1993.

The winter of 1993–94 shattered records for cold temperatures in the East and Midwest, accompanied by unusual accumulations of snow and ice. Eastern bluebirds, with their numbers already lower from the previous year, experienced further weather-related setbacks. In contrast to the declines of 1958 and 1961, this time the core population remains strong enough to recover quickly over several seasons of more favorable weather.

～

Bluebirds chance the vagaries of early-spring storms as they migrate north. In some years they return too early. Photographer Glenn Van Nimwegen visited Flaming Gorge National Recreation Area, Wyoming, in mid-April a few years ago. Gusty winds buffeted the area with snow squalls. Van Nimwegen counted sixty-five mountain bluebirds lined up on the restroom windows, sheltered from the freezing winds.

The following morning, he watched as about three dozen robins scratched and dug in the snow beneath Russian olive trees, retrieving small white seeds. To Van Nimwegen's amazement, mountain bluebirds followed each robin. As robins pulled seeds from the snow, bluebirds plucked them from the robins' beaks. Surprisingly few robins protested, but some grabbed bluebirds by the back and flipped them aside.

Between feeding forays, bluebirds huddled together for warmth. The storm lasted four days. Afterward, Van Nimwegen counted a dozen dead bluebirds. When the snow melted, the robins and the rest of the bluebirds dispersed.

Mountain bluebirds usually reach nesting grounds as much as two weeks before eastern bluebirds reach similar latitudes. Bluebird observer Dave Ahlgren, an airline pilot, predicts the spring return of eastern bluebirds to Minnesota by watching for a weather phenomenon known as a "Texas screamer." The jet stream, which normally flows from west to east, dips low over Texas, then bends sharply north toward Minnesota. Even though conditions on the ground may be calm, winds two thousand feet (610 m) aloft reach speeds of seventy miles per hour (113 kph). Ahlgren believes the bluebirds hitch a ride north. After the snow has melted, Ahlgren predictably sees numbers of bluebirds on the second day of a Texas screamer. His question is: How do the birds know the snow has melted?

Naturalist John Burroughs noticed a similar phenomenon. In the late 1800s, he wrote, "The bluebird enjoys the preeminence of being the first bit of color that cheers our northern landscape. . . . In New York and New England the sap starts up in the sugar maple the very day the bluebird arrives, and sugar-making begins forthwith."

A legend claims that the spring song of the bluebird makes apple trees burst into full bloom. Each spring, some of us are lucky enough to see the brilliant blue of a male bluebird contrasting with the pink of fleeting blossoms. The bluebird has returned. The cycle of the seasons is complete, and the bluebird's sweet song bubbles with the promise of new life.

Above: *Bluebirds molt in late summer when insects and fruits are still abundant enough to provide plenty of energy for feather replacement.* (Juvenile eastern bluebird eating mountain ash berries, photo copyright by Gregory K. Scott)
Left: *Bluebirds from the north live "on the edge." They fly far enough south to avoid the worst winter weather and return early in the spring to claim nesting territories. Occasionally they are caught in unexpected snowstorms.* (Mountain bluebirds, photo copyright by Galen Burrell)

Opposite top: *Winter weather drives bluebirds from northern areas. As insects become scarce, the birds rely on fruits for a larger portion of their diets. (Mountain bluebirds eating juniper berries, photo copyright by Galen Burrell)* Opposite bottom left: *On frigid winter nights, bluebirds conserve energy by sleeping together in tree cavities or nest boxes. (Eastern bluebirds, photo copyright by Michael L. Smith)* Opposite bottom right: *Bluebird populations, especially in eastern North America, decline after harsh winters. These cold, icy winters occur on an average of every ten years. Bluebird numbers usually rebound within three to four years after severe weather. (Photo copyright by Connie Toops)*

Above: *A few years ago, mountain bluebirds returning to southwestern Wyoming were caught in a spring blizzard. Photographer Glenn Van Nimwegen discovered a group of robins scratching through the snow to find Russian olive seeds. He watched in amazement as mountain bluebirds followed each robin and opportunistically grabbed seeds as the robins uncovered them. (Photo copyright by Glenn Van Nimwegen)* Right: *In March 1859, Henry David Thoreau wrote, "The bluebird comes and with his warble drills the ice and sets free the rivers and ponds and frozen ground." (Photo copyright by Steve and Dave Maslowski)*

Bluebird Trails

A Cross-Country Sampler

Minneapolis, Minnesota

During the late 1970s, U.S. Fish and Wild-life Service Breeding Bird Surveys indicated that sightings of eastern bluebirds were un-common to rare in the Upper Midwest. Dick and Vi Peterson had maintained a bluebird trail near their Minnesota home for many years, and as bluebird numbers dwindled, other interested individuals sought their advice on how to help these birds. In 1978 the Petersons worked with the Audubon Chapter of Min-neapolis to organize the Bluebird Recovery Program (BBRP).

The BBRP began with eleven volunteer observers. During their first year, they watched five pairs of east-ern bluebirds and documented twenty-two young birds fledging. News of these bluebird-lovers spread by word-of-mouth and newspaper articles, and amazingly, BBRP membership has grown to some 2,400 people across the United States and Canada. Volunteers present work-shops on how to attract bluebirds. The group publishes a newsletter and other educational materials. Partici-pants reported more than twelve thousand bluebird fledgings in 1993.

A male eastern bluebird perches on the angular style of nest box developed by Dick Peterson. (Photo copyright by Connie Toops)

One of the BBRP's most recent successes is returning bluebirds to the Twin Cities, where they were not seen for half a century. A few years ago, Mary McGee, a BBRP member who lives on Cedar Lake, decided to place bluebird nest boxes along a walking trail near her home. The first year she found room for two boxes. Amazingly, a pair of bluebirds discovered them and fledged five young within sight of downtown Minneapolis.

Ten boxes line the greenway now. Mary has experienced minor setbacks because the trail is so heavily used. "We've found cigarette butts in some of the nest boxes, and a year ago on the Fourth of July, someone attached a pinwheel to one. The box was charred," Mary explained, "but the female hung on and hatched those eggs. They all fledged."

McGee's informational signs have sparked the in-

Although eastern bluebirds were absent from Minneapolis for more than fifty years, a trail of nest boxes near Cedar Lake has enticed them back within sight of the downtown area. (Photo copyright by Dick Peterson)

terest of greenway users, and as they find out more about them, residents are taking pride in the returning birds. In 1993 McGee's heart-of-the-city trail fostered four broods of bluebirds and an equal number of tree swallow nests.

Prothonotary warblers are among the forty species of North American birds that nest in cavities. Like bluebirds, their populations have declined as nesting habitat has disappeared. (Photo copyright by Michael L. Smith)

Competing for Nest Cavities

Bluebirds number among the forty types of North American birds that nest in cavities. Woodpeckers are primary cavity makers. Dagger-sharp beaks and reinforced skulls empower them to chisel into live or dead wood. They normally excavate a new den for each brood. After they leave, secondary cavity nesters, including bluebirds, compete for the vacant holes. Bluebirds also use cavities formed by fires or decay and nest boxes made by humans.

Chickadees, titmice, and nuthatches all inhabit forests. They occasionally occupy bluebird houses placed in wooded locations. While these songbirds do at times evict bluebirds from cavities, bluebirds also evict them. Since the woodland species prefer homes in the forest, and bluebirds choose more open areas, they generally coexist in peace. Chickadees, titmice, and nuthatches nest early and usually raise one brood. Bluebirds may move in after them for second or third nestings.

In Colorado, mountain bluebirds nested in the same tree as pygmy nuthatches. The male nuthatch helped feed babies at both nests. A male eastern bluebird fed young chickadees in a nest about forty feet (12.2 m) from his nest in Minnesota. An eastern bluebird laid eggs in a Carolina chickadee nest in Tennessee. Chickadees raised the bluebirds.

Great-crested flycatchers in the East and ash-throated flycatchers in the West use cavities. They are slightly larger than bluebirds, and thus have trouble squeezing into bluebird houses. They do compete with bluebirds for natural holes. In the Great Basin, mountain bluebirds and ash-throated flycatchers sometimes nest in neighboring cavities in the same juniper snag.

A few years ago researchers in northern Nevada watched a nest box in which a female mountain bluebird laid two eggs; then a pair of ash-throated flycatchers took over the site. With very few additions, the female flycatcher settled onto the bluebird's nest. During the next few days, she added five eggs. All of the eggs hatched, and the flycatchers fed their own babies as well as the orphaned bluebirds. They fledged successfully.

In these unusual cases, there is no biological advantage for a parent to raise young of another species. Such anomalies are best explained by strong—but slightly misguided—hormonal drives to care for young during the nesting season.

Prothonotaries are the only cavity-nesting warblers in the eastern United States. Since they inhabit wet woodlands instead of grassy openings, prothonotary warblers seldom compete with bluebirds for nest sites. But like bluebirds, populations of these lovely golden warblers have declined in the past several decades due to loss of habitat. They will need human assistance if their numbers are to rebound. Nest boxes should be located near swamps and quiet rivers, and openings of 1 1/8-inch (2.9 cm) diameter are appropriate for prothonotaries.

The brown-headed cowbird, common in agricultural regions throughout North America, does not build a nest of its own. Instead, the female sneaks in and lays a speckled egg in another bird's nest. Some victims recognize the intruder's egg and toss it or start a new nest. Many unsuspecting warblers, vireos, and native sparrows, however, tend the larger, faster-maturing baby cowbirds to the neglect of their own young. Cowbirds usually choose open nests instead of cavities. In a few instances, cowbirds have laid eggs in bluebird nests, and all three species of bluebirds have raised cowbird babies. Usually, female bluebirds recognize and abandon clutches parasitized by cowbirds.

A century ago Bewick's wrens lived around fencerows and farms in the East. House wrens were limited to brushy habitats. House wrens have readily adapted to backyard birdhouses and have increased around human habitation. Bewick's wrens rarely co-exist with house wrens. Their populations have declined.

House wrens are only two-thirds as large as bluebirds, but what they lack in size they make up in restless energy and cocky demeanor. They winter in the southern United States, extending south into Central America. Migrant house wrens return about a month after bluebirds. Unless spring weather has been unusually harsh, bluebirds are brooding eggs or may even have young in the nest when wrens begin searching for cavities. This gives bluebirds an early advantage. By May or June when bluebirds renest, wrens challenge them aggressively. House wrens normally raise two broods each year.

Male wrens labor from daylight until dusk, stuffing nest boxes and natural cavities full of twigs. They sing all the while. When a female arrives, the male sings even more ardently and leads her to each of his prospective nests. She selects one and adds a final lining of soft grasses, rootlets, and feathers.

House wrens are extremely intolerant of other species within their territories. They slip into unguarded nests, puncturing or tossing out eggs. They will throw out just-hatched bluebirds. Babies older than two days are too heavy to maneuver, so wrens peck them to death or bury them beneath a barrage of twigs.

Since house wrens drive bluebirds and other cavity nesters away from nests, they often draw the wrath of those who build and tend bluebird boxes. While it is legal to remove unused "dummy" nests, active wren nests and their reddish-brown, speckled eggs are protected by federal law. The best way to avoid conflicts with wrens is to locate boxes for bluebirds away from the brushy, overgrown habitats wrens love.

❧

Colonists learned from Native Americans to hang hollow gourds to attract purple martins. These large swallows eat thousands of airborne insects. Eastern populations of martins have readily adapted to apartment-style birdhouses mounted on tall poles. Western martins, which are a geographically separate race, nest in natural tree cavities. Their populations are declining as habitat disappears.

Bluebirds occasionally venture into a martin colony. Martins usually chase them away, but both have shared the same housing complex. Living arrangements seem most satisfactory when bluebirds find a vacant apartment on a side away from most of the martins.

Two other species of swallows interact with bluebirds in the quest for cavities. Tree swallows inhabit most of North America. Males have iridescent green feathers on their heads, backs, and wings. Underparts are white. Mature females are dull green and white. Back and wing feathers of yearling females are greenish-brown. Tree swallows winter along southern coasts and migrate north about a month later than bluebirds. Bluebirds are fairly secure from swallow competition for the first brood. Rivalry intensifies as bluebirds renest.

Like bluebirds, some tree swallows return to the previous year's nest. Pairs sit on fences or power lines near a cavity, taking turns peeking inside. Nests are constructed of dry grasses and lined with numerous feathers, often collected from nearby barnyards.

Richard Tuttle has studied interactions between eastern bluebirds and tree swallows at Delaware State Park in central Ohio since 1979. Tuttle placed pairs of nest boxes along this bluebird trail. At many, bluebirds and tree swallows nest within twenty feet (6.1 m) of each other.

While photographing a pair of Tuttle's boxes, I witnessed the following encounter. A male tree swallow sat on the roof of the far nest box. Suddenly, a

Where cavities are in short supply, mountain bluebirds have shared the same decaying tree with ash-throated flycatchers or pygmy nuthatches. (Male mountain bluebird, photo copyright by Jeffrey Rich)

male eastern bluebird dove at the swallow, driving it down near the ground. The swallow circled away. The bluebird hovered in front of the entrance as the swallow returned. The bluebird dove again. After the swallow left, the bluebird perched atop the box and sat for a few moments. Then the swallow buzzed the bluebird, and the bluebird moved to the adjacent box. The male swallow landed on his original perch, where a female swallow joined him. All of them remained for a few minutes, as if sizing up a truce.

During the eight years that Tuttle monitored 93 to 117 nest boxes on this trail, he found that tree swallows interrupted the nesting of nine pairs of bluebirds. In the same period, bluebirds pirated eleven tree swallow nests. Swallows were most aggressive in late April and early May, when they were intently searching for nest sites. Bluebirds were already incubating eggs or had young in nests. When swallows seized the boxes, they added nest materials on top of bluebird eggs or young. Bluebird takeovers occurred in late May and early June, coinciding with the time bluebirds were laying eggs for their second broods. The bluebirds buried swallow eggs and young under fresh nest materials when they won boxes.

After Tuttle installed his trail at the park, the tree swallow population increased, but so did bluebird nesting success. Pairing nest boxes also affected competition from house wrens. Swallows defend their nest from other swallows, but they defend a territory fifteen yards (13.7 m) in diameter around the box from competing birds, including wrens and house sparrows.

In a research paper presented in the bluebirding journal *Sialia*, Tuttle explained how bluebirds benefit from having swallows as neighbors, "House wrens sing and flutter from bush to bush as they work their way toward a desired nest box. As they emerge from cover to fly the last leg to the box, one swallow swoop will drive wrens into the nearest bush."

"I've seen pairs of bluebirds," Tuttle continued, "flare their wings and stand in defiance on top of their nest boxes as neighboring and floater swallows join, sometimes in mobs of six or more, trying to drive them away. I've never seen a bluebird retreat from aggressive swallow swoops."

"When I see a pair of bluebirds ducking and flaring their wings as they protect their box from the diving hordes of tree swallows," Tuttle concluded, "I actually cheer them on—both species that is. I've found more harmony than conflict between bluebirds and swallows."

West of the Great Plains, bluebird-swallow interactions are complicated by the addition of violet-green swallows. They are distinguished by large patches of white on the rump. Tree swallows dominate nest sites at lower elevations, but slightly smaller violet-green swallows range upwards to seven thousand feet (2,134 m). They also nest where suitable habitat remains in urban areas, similar to the niche purple martins occupy in the East.

In a study of interactions between bluebirds and swallows southwest of Portland, Oregon, Hubert Prescott and Earl Gillis observed tree swallows competing intensively with western bluebirds for cavities during a week or two in the late spring. Swallows sometimes gather in small groups to intimidate other species away from their territories. Violet-green swallows harass bluebirds over a longer time. In spells of cool, wet weather, the lack of insects draws bluebirds farther from their nests. In their absence, swallows hijack their cavities.

Prescott and Gillis discovered that western bluebirds fledged more young per nest box mounted on large trees than in boxes placed on fence posts. Aerially superior swallows harassed bluebirds in open areas. With their backs protected by the tree trunk or branches, male bluebirds had a competitive advantage. Bluebirders in the East advise against nailing nest boxes to trees because predators such as snakes and raccoons gain easy access. In Oregon, the advantage against swallows outweighs losses to predators at tree-mounted boxes.

Bluebirds do inhabit some western boxes paired with tree or violet-green swallows, and the swallows do defend the area around both boxes against encroaching house wrens and house sparrows. Unusual interactions between western bluebirds and violet-green swallows have been documented. Once in 1981 and twice in 1982, observers near Corvallis, Oregon, found pairs of violet-green swallows assisting in raising western bluebird nestlings. None of the swallows had active nests at the time. The swallows entered bluebird boxes with food, removed fecal sacs, and chased away other violet-green and tree swallows.

If you peek into a bluebird house and find a nest lined with feathers, you will know that tree or violet-green swallows have claimed the box. (Tree swallow nest, photo copyright by Connie Toops)

They did not repel the parent bluebirds, nor did the bluebirds seem unduly upset with the helper swallows.

A possible explanation for the unrelated helpers could be a recent loss of swallow nests or eggs, with these birds still having strong parental instincts. Two of three pairs nested in the boxes immediately after the bluebird young fledged, so the helper status may have assured access to a future nest site.

Proprietors of a bluebird trail north of Calgary, Alberta, twice found nests containing five tree swallow eggs and three mountain bluebird eggs. Both times, tree swallows raised their own young as well as the bluebirds. Since swallow lifestyles and feeding habits differ from those of bluebirds, fostered fledglings probably join nearby families of bluebirds after they leave the nest.

Top inset: *Although only two-thirds the size of bluebirds, feisty male house wrens oust them by singing robustly and stuffing nest cavities full of twigs. (Photo copyright by Connie Toops)*

Center inset: *In the West, bluebirds sometimes share paired nest boxes with violet-green or tree swallows. Swallows may, however, drive bluebirds from exposed boxes. When this happens, western bluebirds seem more successful defending houses mounted on trees. (Photo copyright by Connie Toops)* Bottom inset: *Violet-green swallows inhabit the western United States and Canada. Like bluebirds, they hunt in open fields and nest in cavities. (Photo copyright by Connie Toops)* Above: *Especially in eastern North America, bluebirds benefit when tree swallows are close neighbors. Swallows harass competing house wrens and house sparrows but seldom bother bluebirds. (Photo copyright by Connie Toops)*

Bluebird Trails
A Cross-Country Sampler

Ronan, Montana

I wouldn't have needed directions to find Art Aylesworth in Ronan, Montana. Any local resident could have pointed out the semiretired insurance agent, known as The Bluebird Man of Ronan. Art helped organize Mountain Bluebird Trails, a regional group of bluebird monitors. He has overseen the construction and distribution of twenty-six thousand cedar nest boxes, and he's still going strong.

Art grew up on a farm northwest of Ronan and remembers bluebirds from childhood. "Four or five families that lived close had mailboxes with slots for letters but no dampers over the slots," he recalled. "Bluebirds nested in nearly all of them. They used the twine boxes on grain binders and nooks and crannies around houses and barns."

"We had a blizzard in 1973, and I noticed bluebirds sitting in trees like blue bulbs on a Christmas tree," Art continued. "I wanted to find out how to get them back on the ranch, but it was hit-or-miss at first."

Aylesworth made six standard nest boxes and put them up the next spring. "I got one pair," he smiled. "So I put out another six boxes. I still had one pair." Undaunted, he built 1,200 boxes and mounted them on fence posts from Ronan fifty miles (80.5 km) southwest to Saint Regis. When the boxes attracted no bluebirds, most of his helpers lost interest. "No one wants to

do the work with no rewards," he confided.

Art kept trying. There were precious few bluebirds left, but several discovered his offerings. Still, it bothered him that such a small percentage of boxes were being used. In 1979 he met Duncan Mackintosh, who experienced similar poor results with a mountain bluebird trail in Alberta. Both commented on how the birds investigated the boxes each spring but then ignored them.

A few weeks later Art studied a male mountain bluebird as it courted a female. "The male and female were at the box and the male wanted to show her, but he just couldn't squeeze inside," Art recalled. "There was another pair nesting nearby, but the male's feathers were very ruffled, especially around the shoulders. Then it dawned on me—maybe the holes were too small."

Aylesworth consulted Mackintosh. Coincidentally, Mackintosh had made similar observations in Alberta that same week. They concluded that the 1 1/2-inch (3.8 cm) openings in eastern bluebird nest boxes would not accommodate larger mountain bluebirds. They agreed to test entrances of 1 5/8 inches (4.1 cm) in Alberta and openings of 1 9/16 inches (4 cm) on Aylesworth's boxes. Starlings immediately invaded the 1 5/8-inch holes, so Mackintosh also sized down to 1 9/16 inches.

Aylesworth enlarged box openings all along his trail. "We immediately doubled our nesting success," he remembered. "We also began making the boxes bigger, since we were seeing both western and mountain bluebirds with as many as ten eggs and nestlings per box.

The ones the North American Bluebird Society promoted for eastern bluebirds were just too small."

❦

This was a cool July afternoon. Wisps of gray clouds hung on the ten-thousand-foot (3,050-m) Mission Peaks east of Ronan, crowning their beauty. "Let's look at some of the trail," Art suggested. We headed west in his pickup, emblazoned "Bluebird Man" on the front. We turned onto a gravel road that winds along the Flathead River. Every quarter mile (0.4 km) were nest boxes. As Art drove, his practiced eyes scanned for bluebirds. He delighted in pointing them out.

"The last roundup of wild bison took place right there," Art said, gesturing to the far side of the Flathead. "This is one of the first places I put up boxes. A local rancher pulled up and asked me what I was doing. When I told him, the look on his face said he thought I'd lost my mind. It was a heck of a job to keep up all those boxes myself, plus run a business. I came close to giving up on the bluebirds more than once."

To the south were thirty miles (48.3 km) of mountain bluebird trails and twenty miles (32.2 km) of western bluebird trails. "Mountain bluebirds," Art said, "use both timbered and nontimber lands from about two to ten thousand feet (610–3,050 m). They return long before the tree swallows, so they have their pick of boxes in the spring. Forty to 60 percent nest a second time. It's rare, but we do have a few with three broods," Aylesworth explained. Western bluebirds are found near ponderosa pines. Art believes the fragrant, insect-laden bitterbrush shrubs growing with the pines attract them.

We encountered half a dozen vehicles on this dusty lane. As each passed, Art's right hand waved casually, recognizing friends and clients. Many belong to his bluebird network. The news that bluebirds were finally using Art's boxes spread from farm to farm. Before long, folks from several counties had requested nest boxes.

"We have about forty-five volunteers who help build boxes," he explained. "A local mill, Plum Creek Lumber, donates cedar trim boards. I call eight to fifteen volunteers, and we meet at someone's farm shop or the lo-

Art Aylesworth dreams of bringing bluebirds back to the abundance he remembers from childhood. (Photo copyright by Connie Toops)

cal college. We do this in the winter when it's snowy and cold and we need a social outing. We work from seven to eleven at night. Two nights we cut pieces, then we get a new crew and spend two more nights assembling them. The least we've ever done in a session is five hundred boxes. Usually we're up around two thousand."

We have reached Highway 200 near Dixon. "This is part of our Montana Centennial Trail," Art explained. "Dennis Flath, the nongame coordinator, got the idea of a bluebird trail that would go from east to west across the state. That's about seven hundred miles [1,126 km]. We used 3,380 boxes." Construction began two years ahead of the 1989 celebration. County extension agents and 4-H clubs helped mount and monitor the nest boxes. "We're always looking for low-cost ways to do this," Art commented, "so we sent boxes out with seed trucks, cattle trucks, oil tankers, and kids going back to college. Other kids would pick them up and take them on home."

As we circled back to Ronan, I asked the Bluebird Man what part of this project had been most satisfying. I expected he would mention the 16,045 bluebirds fledged the previous summer. Instead, he replied, "It's fun to watch the excitement of other people getting involved."

Art thought for a moment and added, "Real success? Well, remember the rancher who saw me out there years ago putting up boxes and thought I was crazy? He came up to me about five years later and said, 'Say, Art, have you got any more of those bluebird boxes?' Now that's success."

Pests and Predators

We lived for several years in northeastern Mississippi, a bluebirder's mecca. With scattered trees, a small pond across the road, and surrounding lawns and short-grass fields, our location provided perfect habitat. Bluebirds perched on the utility wires near our house. We invited them into the yard with nest boxes and a birdbath, and we encountered few problems from blowflies, house sparrows, or cats.

Pests and predators can complicate life for bluebirds and their hosts. Parasitic blowflies (*Protocalliphora sialia*) weaken nestlings in cool, wet years when food is scarce. Blowfly larvae, which resemble gray maggots, attach to young birds at night and suck their blood. They hide in nest materials by day, but small scabs on the chicks reveal their presence. Blowfly larvae change into cigar-shaped brown pupae that fall to the bottom of the box. Adults hatch in two weeks. These red-eyed flies lay eggs in other bluebird nests.

Some bluebird monitors recommend treating infected boxes with pyrethrin-based insecticides (such as Flys Away II, developed to keep flies from bothering horses). But insecticides also kill tiny jewel wasps (*Nasonia*) that parasitize many of the blowflies, keeping their populations in check naturally. An alternate method of combating blowflies is to replace infected nests with clean ones made from dry grass or with nests saved from previous years. Parent bluebirds do not seem to object. Foster *Nasonia* wasps by

dropping infected nests into a large bucket. Cover the top with 1/8-inch (0.3-cm) screening. Jewel wasps escape as they mature, but larger blowflies are trapped.

Now and then paper wasps commandeer a box. At temperatures below 50 degrees Fahrenheit (10° C), they are too cold to fly, so nests can be removed. Wasps can also be killed with pyrethrin sprays. Rubbing the inside top of the box with petroleum jelly may deter future nest attachment.

Ants will infect nest boxes, especially if an egg has broken or a nestling has died. Some bluebirders claim a clove or two of garlic placed at the base of the post repels ants. Others employ Tanglefoot, available at garden supply stores. Since this sticky substance will also trap curious chickadees and other small birds, use it sparingly. One narrow wrap below the grease coating on a metal mounting pole will suffice.

Constrictor snakes, especially rat snakes in the East and Midwest and bull snakes in the Central Plains and West, are regular predators of bluebirds. A study of black rat snakes in Arkansas concluded that they forage along fencerows and prey on eggs or young bluebirds both by day and at night. Snakes are agile climbers. They slither in, squeeze and swallow their prey, digest for a short while, and then leave the empty but otherwise undisrupted nest. Parent birds are reluctant to enter a cavity if they have seen a snake there.

Blue jays, magpies, and starlings pluck young

The requirements for attracting bluebirds include an open lawn or meadow where they can hunt, a dependable source of water, and a safe place to nest. (Male western bluebird, photo copyright by Hugh P. Smith, Jr.)

Above: *By day, blowfly larvae hide in bluebird nest materials. At night they crawl onto baby birds and suck their blood. (Photo copyright by Gregory K. Scott)* Left: *Constrictor snakes prey on songbird eggs and babies. Repel them by installing a metal guard beneath the nest box or waxing metal mounting poles. (Photo copyright by Connie Toops)*

birds from natural cavities with holes large enough to allow them in. Kestrels, Cooper's hawks, and magpies occasionally grab a nestling that lingers near the entrance or a newly fledged bird. Nest box roof designs that allow an ample overhang in front discourage magpie predation. Magpies will also hammer woodpecker-style to enlarge a nest box opening. Only one or two of the young may disappear to bird predators. Parents will continue to raise the rest of the brood.

White-footed mice and deer mice sometimes settle into bluebird boxes during the winter. They often finish nesting before bluebirds return. If boxes retain strong odors from mouse urine, air them out well. Deter mice by cleaning boxes in the fall, then leaving the door open for the winter. If you close boxes to provide winter bluebird roosts, recheck them in the spring to remove mouse debris.

Now and then a mouse will nibble on bluebird eggs or nestlings occupying their old nests. But squirrels and chipmunks are more likely to cause problems. They gnaw to enlarge entrance holes, sometimes eating eggs or taking over the nest site. Avoid attaching boxes next to diagonal fence braces, which are highways for climbing predators. Foil them by attaching an inverted metal cone or predator baffle to the mounting post. Metal plates with cutouts the diameter of the entrance can be tacked on box fronts to keep rodents and woodpeckers from enlarging the hole.

Raccoons are troublesome predators of bluebirds. They are intelligent and widespread in both rural and suburban habitats. Raccoons prowl fencerows and the edges of woodlands. They readily climb trees, wooden posts, and many metal posts on which nest boxes are mounted. With a ten-inch (25.4-cm) reach, their probing paws can grab eggs, chicks, or even the brooding female. Coons remember successes and soon return to raid nearby nest boxes. Telltale signs of raccoon visits are nest material pulled through the entrance and claw marks on boxes. A thick coat of bearing grease applied to the middle third of a metal pole discourages them. They also have great difficulty climbing slick metal poles buffed with carnauba wax. If children play near the boxes, their parents will prefer the latter method!

The Noel guard, devised by Jim Noel of Ashland, Illinois, is a tunnel of wire mesh hardware cloth that can be attached to a house after nesting begins. (Adult bluebirds may be reluctant to enter the wire tunnel before they lay eggs.) Outward-pointing wires poke the legs and paws of raccoons or cats that try to reach into the nest. This guard is a very effective deterrent to furry predators.

If you tend a bluebird box or landscape your yard to attract bluebirds, sooner or later you will encounter cats. Their favorite lurking places include birdbaths, bird feeders, and nest boxes. Sleeping bluebirds, nesting females, and inattentive fledglings are easy targets. Humans domesticated cats centuries ago because they were efficient killers of rodents in stored crops. Farmers still keep cats for that reason. Even owners of house pets brag of their cats' hunting prowess. How much impact do these nonnative cats have on wildlife?

Cats hunt instinctively, whether hungry or not. They are stealthy killers in both daylight and darkness. Barn-raised cats, feral cats, and house pets on brief visits outside all catch mice, voles, shrews, small rabbits, and a variety of songbirds. A study in England revealed that the nation's five million cats kill seventy million small animals annually. Twenty million of these are birds. Research in Wisconsin concluded that nineteen million songbirds per year are wiped out by that state's cats. The cat population in the United States numbers between fifty and sixty million. If they kill at a rate similar to that of British cats, more than six hundred thousand birds a day in this country perish in feline jaws.

What can you do? If the pet is yours, have it spayed or neutered. The Humane Society estimates thirty-five thousand kittens are born every day in the United States. (For perspective, only ten thousand human babies are born daily in this nation.) Unwanted cats become feral consumers of wildlife.

The best option is to keep cats indoors, away from birds. If you are plagued by feral cats, call the animal control warden to trap and remove them. In the short term, you can scare the offending cat by making loud noises or employing a long-range squirt gun each time you chase it away. If you need to convince neighbors to control their pets, share these facts. Free-roaming cats live three to five years, while in-house cats reach twice or three times that age. Free-roaming cats are exposed to fleas, ticks, worms, pesticides, and diseases such as distemper, rabies, feline leukemia, and feline immunodeficiency virus (an AIDS-like disease). The greatest hazard to outdoor cats is being killed or injured by a vehicle. As long as cats receive enough attention so they are not bored, they will contentedly live indoors. Owners will prolong their lives and save on expensive veterinary bills by keeping them inside.

∽

We now realize certain mammals, birds, insects, and plants evolved in specific localities, governed by evolutionary checks and balances to control their abundance. But this concept of ecology was poorly understood until recently. Previously, people imported species from around the world without any thought of how they would interact with native species.

Clubs such as the American Acclimatization Society of New York sponsored novelty wildlife introductions in the late 1800s. Under the leadership of drug manufacturer Eugene Schieffelin, this group imported a few of each of the species of birds mentioned in Shakespeare's plays. During 1890 and 1891, more than a hundred starlings were freed in Central Park.

For most Shakespearean birds—such as nightingales and skylarks—the habitats, climate, and food sources of North America were too different from those of their homeland. They soon perished. But cities in North America are much like cities in Europe, and starlings fared well. Within fifty years, their descendants formed what Roger Tory Peterson remembered as "black blizzards of birds," with flocks of thirty thousand or more swarming about the ledges of buildings in New York City. Starlings reached the West Coast by 1950. They now rank among the most numerous birds in North America.

House sparrows represent a similarly ironic success story. Ancestral house sparrows inhabited Eurasian savannas and adapted to the easy lifestyle of feeding on spilled grain and livestock wastes near human settlement. They found crevices around buildings perfect for stuffing with sprawling nests of straw and feathers. As domestic agriculture spread across Europe and North Africa, so did ever-expanding populations of house sparrows.

Covies of these drab birds were imported and released in the United States several times beginning in the early 1850s. Promoters claimed they would eat cankerworms on shade trees. The diary of French composer Jacques Offenbach contains this passage from an 1876 visit to New York City, "From my window I can see in Madison Square a curious and charming detail. On the upper branches of the trees have been put little boxes half hidden among the leaves. They are for the sparrows recently brought from Europe. These little exiled birds are the objects of every kind of attention . . . they are respected like the pigeons of Saint-Marc."

It did not take long for house sparrows to fall from favor. They thrived in cities, dining on partially digested grains deposited on streets plied by horse carts. They invaded farms, gobbling cereals from fields and storage bins, while spreading weed seeds in their droppings. They followed the railroads west, consuming grain that spilled from boxcars. House sparrows arrived on the West Coast in the late 1800s.

Exotic starlings and house sparrows exploited native bluebirds by nesting in cavities. Being larger and highly aggressive, starlings have no trouble seizing woodpecker holes and natural openings. They have even been seen evicting kestrels and screech owls from nests. A Colorado observer watched a starling harass a nest-drilling flicker by grabbing the flicker's neck in its beak and latching onto its back. During their last encounter, the starling held the struggling flicker in its grip for thirty minutes. When the flicker finally broke free, it deserted the den and the starling moved in. Starlings cannot squeeze into openings smaller than 1 9/16 inches (4 cm) in diameter, so properly sized holes on bluebird nest boxes will exclude them.

House sparrows nest not only in natural cavities and bird houses, but under eaves, behind shutters, over light fixtures, and in barns and agricultural buildings. Since they can squeeze into holes 1 1/8 inches (2.9 cm) in diameter, there is no sure way to keep them from entering bluebird nest boxes.

Male house sparrows are extremely pugnacious while trying to attract mates. They will usurp the nests of bluebirds, wrens, chickadees, and other songbirds by breaking or throwing out eggs, killing nestlings, and occasionally killing adult birds. If a male spar-

Above: *Squirrels sometimes gnaw their way into bluebird boxes. Attach a metal plate with a hole sized for bluebirds over the front of the box to discourage squirrels. (Photo copyright by Connie Toops) Left: The Noel guard, a tunnel of hardware cloth with sharp points projecting from the outer edges, effectively keeps cats and raccoons from reaching inside a nest box. (Photo copyright by Connie Toops)*

row cannot enter the tiny opening on a wren or chickadee box, it may perch on top and drive approaching adults away.

House sparrows are adaptable and prolific. As use of draft animals ended and agricultural practices modernized, sparrow populations began to decline. They compensated by roaming urban parking lots, picking impaled insects from car radiators and gleaning food scraps at fast-food restaurants. A male sparrow may defend as many as five potential nest sites and can support two female mates at the same time. Females raise two (rarely three) broods per season, averaging five young per brood.

Sparrows wreak havoc on bluebirds. Trail monitors know the evidence too well—an adult bluebird found dead in or near the box, with head feathers gone, revealing deep gashes in the skull, and often with eyes pecked out. Although usually the male sparrow attacks, sometimes the female will sneak in while adults are away. A nest that formerly held plump, healthy chicks becomes the site of a massacre. The lifeless bluebirds are pecked, bloodied, mutilated, sometimes dragged from the nest. If they remain in the box, they are usually buried under the debris of the sparrow's new nest.

House sparrows and bluebirds did not evolve on the same continent. It is only through misguided human interference that sparrows rival bluebirds for nesting space. In this competition, house sparrows win unless humans intervene. House sparrows are fairly sedentary. They actively defend a small territory around their nest, fanning out within a mile or two to feed. If you can alleviate house sparrows from nesting sites, you can provide a "safe zone" for bluebirds.

Alien house sparrows are not subject to laws that protect native birds. It is legal to remove them and their nests. As for what to do after you catch them, opinions differ. For people who normally love birds, killing one is an unnatural act. Yet anyone who hopes to return bluebirds to suburban and agrarian areas needs to make a personal decision about house sparrows.

"Environmentalism is a matter of hard choices," wrote ornithologist Rick Blom. Simply releasing house sparrows somewhere else may result in their invasion of other bluebird habitat. The quickest way to dispatch house sparrows is to wring their necks. Corpses can be donated to wildlife rehabilitators, who feed them to birds of prey. People who cannot kill sparrows in hand have gassed them with car exhaust, drowned them, or placed them, bagged in plastic, in the freezer.

Although there are so many house sparrows that the task may seem daunting at first, it is possible to eradicate them from a neighborhood. That is exactly what Joe Huber has accomplished around his home in Heath, Ohio.

Joe's first encounter with house sparrows was as a youngster, trapping and removing them from the henhouse when they flocked to the chicken feed. Years later, Joe put up a martin house. Sparrows moved in. Huber also had bluebird boxes in his yard for which sparrows competed. Remembering childhood successes at the chicken coop, he decided to trap the sparrows. Joe exchanged letters and ideas with many experienced martin and bluebird hosts. By the early 1970s he was experimenting with various styles of traps.

Joe led me into his backyard and picked up a weathered bird box. "This must have been made by someone right out of engineering school," Huber commented, touching a Rube Goldberg mechanism. A weighted trip bar triggered a plate that pivoted in a slot. "But it gave me the idea for my in-the-box trap," he explained.

Huber is tall and slender, with graying hair. His shop overflows with woodworking tools, labeled bins of hardware, and nest boxes in various stages of assembly. He constantly mulls new ideas to improve his traps and bluebird boxes.

Joe showed me a progression of designs for a sparrow trap that can slip into any bluebird house. The trap is mounted on thin plywood. It attaches by a wire clip, a screw, Velcro, or a magnet, depending on the type of box. He has also perfected a nest box with a built-in sparrow trap that can be activated whenever necessary.

The principle is the same for built-in or retrofit model. When the sparrow flies through the entrance,

A century ago starlings were introduced to North America as a novelty. They have reproduced so efficiently that they now rank among the most abundant birds on this continent. Unfortunately, starlings evict bluebirds from natural nesting cavities. Huge flocks of these nonnative birds consume many of the berries bluebirds rely on for winter food. (Photo copyright by Connie Toops)

it trips a wire bar that causes a metal plate to fall and block the entrance. Of course a bluebird could inadvertently trip the mechanism, so Joe only sets the trap when sparrows are present. He recommends checking it every half hour.

Then Joe shared his secret of ridding the neighborhood of these pesky birds. "Once you catch a sparrow or two in the box, put them in one of these big traps," Joe advised, pointing to a large wire basket with one-way entrances on both sides. "Give them a little grain and water, and let them chirp away. Sparrows love to be with other sparrows, so before you know it, you may have a dozen or more in there."

"I loan a trap to folks along my bluebird trail," Huber explained, "and the decoy birds draw in sparrows from all around." Huber has a friend who captured 1,025 house sparrows in his garden using a similar device. Previously, Joe has removed as many as three hundred house sparrows a year from his neighborhood. That number has dwindled lately as he has depleted their populations. So far this spring, Joe has captured only eleven.

Instead of the incessant, monotonous chirps of male house sparrows so common to Ohio in the spring, the chatter of purple martins and the occasional chur of an eastern bluebird serenade Joe's neighborhood. They are a testimonial to Huber's diligent antisparrow campaign.

House sparrows were also imported from Europe, and, like starlings, they proliferated throughout the United States and Canada at the expense of native species. Male house sparrows do not tolerate other birds within their territories. They often kill adult and baby bluebirds. (Photo copyright by Connie Toops) Inset: Using both in-the-box and ground traps, Joe Huber has systematically eliminated house sparrows from his neighborhood. (Photo copyright by Connie Toops)

Bluebird Trails

A Cross-Country Sampler

Stephanie Wood, a natural resource specialist for the U.S. Forest Service, checks a box containing a mountain bluebird nest. (Photo copyright by Connie Toops)

Beaverhead National Forest, Montana

Among the many places in Montana that Art Aylesworth's boxes have been used are trails in Beaverhead National Forest, south of Sheridan. Stephanie Wood, a natural resource specialist for the U.S. Forest Service, recalled, "In 1988 I saw a note in our Audubon newsletter about free bluebird boxes. I loaded my station wagon up twice—a hundred boxes—and installed them along three trails I monitored in the Virginia City area."

"Two years ago, in connection with my job," Wood continued, "I set up trails above Ruby Reservoir and along Sweetwater Road. Volunteers help me monitor them." Like Aylesworth, Stephanie cleans and repairs the boxes early each spring. She tries to inspect nesting progress twice in May, again in late June or July during second nestings, and if time allows she makes a follow-up visit in the fall.

I joined her on a check of the Ruby Reservoir boxes in early July. We followed a meandering road through a grassy valley, then rose onto sage-covered hills above the lake, where the trail began. The deep blue of the Montana sky was reflected in an even deeper blue of the water. Beyond us were the imposing peaks of the Snowcrest Range. I decided if there is a bluebird heaven, this must be part of it.

"Mountain bluebirds seem to need to be near the water and practically demand a clear view, with only a few trees around," Stephanie said. "The more open the country, the better success we've had." Earlier this year on the Sweetwater Trail, seventeen of the nineteen boxes were occupied by mountain bluebirds. The other two had tree swallows in them. Forty-four of the forty-eight boxes on the Ruby River trail were used by mountain bluebirds. "Some of the ranchers have become rather possessive of the boxes," she reported. "They want to know the success rates, and some have added similar boxes to extend the trails onto their property. The Forest Service is delighted with the response and the requests for box plans. It's wonderful when people see the value of many different species."

One of the bluebird trails in Beaverhead National Forest begins in the sage-covered hills above Ruby Reservoir. (Photo copyright by Connie Toops)

Unraveling
the Mysterious Decline

Bluebird populations—especially those of eastern and western bluebirds—decreased dramatically in the mid-1900s. Frequently cited explanations include indiscriminate use of pesticides and competition from European starlings and house sparrows, both introduced more than a century ago. These certainly influenced bluebirds, but population declines occurred for more complex reasons.

The impacts of pesticides on bluebirds are hard to prove. While DDT was still being used to treat tussock moth infestations in the Pacific Northwest, the U. S. Forest Service studied residual amounts in western and mountain bluebirds. In a 1977 report, scientists concluded that bluebirds were not directly affected by DDT. The compound did, however, kill many insects in addition to tussock moths, reducing insect prey available to the birds. DDT has been banned, but other insecticides sprayed broadly to control "problem" insects continue to reduce the prey base. Adult bluebirds will abandon their nestlings when they cannot find enough food for them.

The insecticide Furadan (carbofuran) is applied to corn and rice to reduce nematode and insect outbreaks. It has been linked to poisonings of birds of prey and songbirds, including eastern bluebirds, in twenty-three states. Furadan is being phased out in the United States, but the chemical is widely promoted and sold abroad. Diazinon, used for insect control on lawns and golf courses, has been linked to deaths of two dozen species of birds in this country. It remains widely available.

Deaths of bluebird nestlings have been documented after the herbicide Roundup was used in the vicinity of nest boxes. Poisoned nestlings died because they could not regulate their body temperatures as they should have been able to do after the female stopped brooding them.

Numerous monitors suspect chemical poisonings when they find adult bluebirds slumped over the nest with wings outstretched. Possible causes include treatment of nearby lawns by chemical care services, fogging lawns for flea and tick control, or liberal use of chemicals in gardens. On farms, bluebirders have noted a "drunken" behavior and slow death of adult bluebirds at the time of late spring chemical applications to nearby alfalfa fields. In all of these cases, the birds are apparently killed by ingesting tainted insects. Birds that die from suspected chemical poisonings should be collected, if possible, and sent quickly to state environmental agencies to be tested.

Not all chemicals are harmful. Bluebirds in California and Oregon successfully use vineyards as feed-

According to a U.S. Fish and Wildlife survey, mountain bluebird populations have increased in the Prairie Provinces and Great Basin but have decreased in the Southwest, California, and British Columbia. (Male mountain bluebird, photo copyright by Jeffrey Rich)

Pesticides used on lawns and golf courses have been linked to deaths of various songbirds, including bluebirds. (Photo copyright by Connie Toops)

Bluebirds require meadows with scattered trees for nest sites and hunting perches. Ideal bluebird habitat dwindles as clearings grow up into brush and dense forest. (Photo copyright by Connie Toops)

ing and nesting areas even though grapevines are sprayed regularly with fungicides. Still, bluebird hosts should consider the potential for pesticide use near boxes during the nesting season. Check with owners of golf courses and commercial orchards to learn what chemicals they employ and when they will be used before installing bluebird trails nearby. If using pesticides in your own yard, always follow manufacturer's directions for rate and method of application. Avoid them when young birds are in the nest.

～

Henry David Thoreau's diary for September 29, 1842, contains the notation, "Today . . . the bluebirds young and old, have revisited their box." His comment confirms that for at least 150 years, people have put out birdhouses around their homes and gardens to attract bluebirds. But in Thoreau's era, bluebird nest boxes were not as vital to the survival of eastern, western, and mountain bluebirds as they are now. To understand why, we must visualize ecological changes that have taken place in North America during the past two centuries.

In 1700 most of the 250,000 colonists lived on the eastern fringe of the continent, within fifty miles (80.5 km) of the coast. At this time, eastern bluebirds inhabited grassy areas that occurred naturally in the East and Midwest as well as those opened by Native Americans' use of fire to promote hunting and berry gathering. Bluebirds required a few trees near these meadows for nest sites. Along rivers and streams, they often nested where branches had rotted from cottonwood and willow trees.

By 1800, settlers had hacked their way west to the Ohio Valley. In virgin forests there, oaks and chestnuts towered eighty feet (24.4 m) to the first branch, while walnuts and tulip poplars grew with trunks six or seven feet (1.8–2.1 m) thick. Settlers girdled trees but left many standing. They planted crops where sunlight penetrated around the massive trunks.

Eastern bluebirds moved into these openings in the forest and became familiar companions around pioneer gardens and orchards. They probably benefited from the settlers' revulsion of "chicken hawks," which were shot on sight. Otherwise, these raptors might have preyed on bluebirds.

John White of Urbana, Illinois, studies presettlement ecology by reading county histories and surveyors' notes. Although comments on specific birds are not prevalent in these documents, he has concluded, "Grassland birds such as cowbirds and dickcissels became more abundant in the eastern part of the United States as the woodlands were cleared by European settlers." Barn owls prospered when midwestern forests were converted to hay meadows. Eastern bluebird numbers also probably increased during this period.

Over the years, this trend in transforming the landscape reversed. Pioneers discontinued the burning that Native Americans used to enhance meadows for deer and berry crops. They suppressed natural lightning fires. White continued, "The most widely remarked natural phenomenon in the writings of early European settlers in Illinois was prairie fire. The second most widely remarked phenomenon was how quickly some of the prairies and open woods grew up into forest as soon as the fires were halted. Areas with little undergrowth developed dense understories and the dense brush supported an increase in species such as ruffed grouse and brown thrashers." Since bluebirds need grassy areas to hunt successfully, their food sources dwindled and their populations declined.

Before settlement, land in the eastern half of the nation was not a huge, uniform forest. Steve Packard of the Illinois Nature Conservancy believes at one time the Midwest was dotted with thirty million acres (12 million hectares) of savanna, or barrens. These wooded plains grew scattered oaks, tolerant of periodic fires and occasional drought. Beneath them flourished a mix of grasses and wildflowers. There were plenty of grasshoppers and other insects, numerous perches to hunt from, and ready cavities where old branches decayed. Eastern bluebirds occupied a perfect niche there.

Westward-moving pioneers rejoiced when they came to savannas. The land was clear enough to plant crops and graze livestock, yet there was sturdy oak timber to build homes, barns, and fences. Harvesting the trees destroyed bluebird nest sites. Compared to the former grassy cover, row crops such as corn and wheat offered poor hunting for hungry bluebirds.

"This is a major ecosystem that has been lost not

Above: Mountain bluebirds thrive in areas recently burned by forest fires. They use fire-scarred trees as nest sites and perch on standing snags to scan the grassy understory for insects. (Photo copyright by Jeffrey Rich) Top inset: U.S. Fish and Wildlife Service records indicate that western bluebird populations in Colorado, Montana, and Washington have increased slightly, but losses in California, Arizona, and Idaho contributed to an overall decline in their numbers during the 1980s. (Photo copyright by Connie Toops)

Bottom inset: *Bluebirds do not prosper after widespread clear-cutting, but western bluebirds do frequent small clearings that have been replanted with seedlings or are used to grow Christmas trees. (Photo copyright by Connie Toops)*

87

only on the ground, but also to people's memory," Packard stated. In most of the Midwest, all that remains of these savannas are obscure names such as Oak Openings, near Toledo, Ohio, or Somme Prairie Grove and Simpson Township Barrens in Illinois. In such areas, where the Nature Conservancy has experimentally cleared the understory and returned fire to the ecosystem, Packard cited the resurgence of eastern bluebirds as "dramatic."

Richard Tuttle, who has studied bluebirds in Ohio since 1968, theorizes that they also used early successional habitats around beaver ponds. Before being trapped out by European settlers, beavers dammed small streams in the Midwest. As water pooled behind the beaver dams, it killed trees whose roots were inundated. Woodpeckers fed and nested in the snags. Tree swallows and bluebirds moved into vacant cavities. Insect food was abundant. Nesting over water safeguarded bluebirds from tree-climbing predators such as rat snakes and raccoons. Since young bluebirds can fly a hundred feet (30 m) or so on maiden flights, they easily reached shore when they fledged. Tuttle has successfully placed bluebird nest boxes on posts in shallow ponds, simulating the beaver pond habitat.

After the Civil War, a new wave of settlers headed west to homestead land claims. By the late 1800s, 80 percent of the virgin forest east of the Mississippi River had been harvested or converted to agricultural land. Much of the prairie in the American heartland had been plowed and planted to row crops. Some of this land, however, was not suited to farming. During the 1930s, tons of topsoil blew away. The Dust Bowl and the Great Depression caused many family farmers to abandon land in the Midwest and South. Eventually these tracts grew up in scrubby second-growth trees. As suitable feeding habitat disappeared, bluebird populations declined.

In the West, timber harvesting and intensive grazing of cattle and sheep began to change the landscape early in this century. Old-timers in western states recall that timbering was once a selective, small-scale operation. Trees were dropped by teams of lumberjacks with crosscut saws. Sawyers stood on springboards inserted into notches ten or fifteen feet (3–4.6 m) up on the tree trunk to avoid cutting the buttressed bases. The huge stumps were left standing, as were big fir trees that had been whipped about in the wind, causing a wood weakness known as "butt shake." Lightning-struck trees, or "pitchtops," were also spared. All of these snags attracted woodpeckers, which riddled the wood with holes. Bluebirds followed them.

Journals of early naturalists contain occasional references to habitats of western bluebirds. They were common in fire-scarred coniferous forests and around dead trees left in clearings, especially where Lewis' woodpeckers and northern flickers had been active. Copses of blue, black, or white oak trees that grew in grassy foothills provided favorite nesting and feeding areas. Western bluebirds also inhabited river valleys with open understories. They nested in decayed limbs of sycamore and black cottonwood trees.

Observers associated mountain bluebirds with high elevations, especially in recently burned zones or near stunted conifers on upper slopes of the Rockies and Cascades. The birds also frequented groves of mountain mahogany, piñon pine, and juniper in the Great Basin region. In wetter montane areas, they were found among aspen trees or in dead timber near streams and lakes.

As western forests came under federal jurisdiction or that of private timber companies, wildfires were suppressed. Like their eastern cousins, western and mountain bluebirds seek early successional habitats. They thrive on insects found in the grassy understory created by recent fires. They nest in the crevices of fire-scarred tree trunks or in woodpecker drillings in fire-killed saplings. As fires were quelled, the mosaic they and insects had created grew up into dense forest. Some bluebirds found nesting and feeding areas near small clearings that retained a few dead trees. Widespread clear-cutting, facilitated by modern chain saws and harvesting machinery, has reduced habitat available to them.

During the dry summer of 1988, a million acres (400,000 hectares) in and around Yellowstone National Park, Wyoming, on which fires had been suppressed for years, were swept by flames. How did that affect bluebird populations?

According to biologist Terry McEneaney, "We see a fair amount of bluebird use after every burn, but bluebird use is best where fires are most intense. The mountain bluebird population has increased substantially in these burns. They will do well as long as there are standing snags, but populations won't stay high forever. Bluebird numbers will gradually decrease as the snags fall over as a result of decayed roots and severe windstorms."

◃◈▹

Agricultural practices have also changed the scene for all three species of bluebirds. Until the wide availability of gasoline-powered tractors, farm work was done by hand or using draft animals. Family farms supported diversity lacking in modern monocultures. In the old days, an eighty-acre (32-hectare) spread would have included pasture, row crops, woodlot, orchard, and garden.

Orchards were not sprayed and pruned to the extent they are today. As limbs of sprawling apple trees died, downy and hairy woodpeckers arrived to dine on wood-boring insects. They chiseled cozy nest holes, which were relinquished to bluebirds, titmice, and chickadees after one woodpecker brood. Arthur C. Bent wrote in his *Life Histories of North American Thrushes, Kinglets and Their Allies*, "from 1880 to 1900, we always looked for bluebirds' nests in natural cavities in apple trees in old orchards, and fully 80 percent of our nests were found in such situations."

Old-time fences were locust posts supporting woven wire or rails of split oak and chestnut. Birds perched on the fences and deposited seeds such as blackberry, poke, and poison ivy. In those days, mow-ing machines left a swath along the fences. The tangle of weeds fed and sheltered insects, birds, and small mammals. Bluebirds nested in rotting posts and dined on the berries and bugs. Houses, barns, and outbuildings of that era—often constructed of logs—offered sheltered recesses where bluebirds nested.

Many contemporary farmers consider fencerows a waste of space. Monoculture fields do not need to be separated as the old pastures and row crops did. Weed killers are liberally sprayed along any fencing that remains. Fields often lie barren through the winter months, providing no food or cover for wildlife.

The number of acres presently in crop production has declined to 80 percent of the area farmed in 1944. Many marginal fields, especially in the Northeast and South, have grown up in brush or trees. At the same time, urban land has doubled, with sprawling tracts of homes and shopping centers gobbling up the rural countryside.

Bluebirds benefited from the land clearing of settlement in the East and from small-scale logging in the West. Their numbers peaked in the mid- to late 1800s. Then fire suppression, growth of cleared lands into scrubby brush, less wildlife-friendly agricultural practices, and loss of nesting sites to alien starlings and sparrows combined to reduce bluebird populations. Were it not for the assistance of humans, who place nest boxes in suitable habitat, bluebirds could now belong to threatened or endangered categories of wildlife.

Corvallis, Oregon

Although Montana bluebirders put out as many nest boxes as they can and are usually rewarded with high occupancy rates, Oregonians monitoring western bluebirds subscribe to the "up-close-and-personal" style of management. I spent two days last summer exploring the back roads of Benton County with Elsie Eltzroth, who organized the Corvallis bluebird trail as a project for the Bicentennial in 1976.

Elsie and other Audubon members mounted eighty-six boxes on fence posts and scattered trees near gardens, pastures, Christmas tree farms, and clear-cuts that first year. Despite the group's enthusiasm, success was elusive. Only one pair of western bluebirds nested and fledged chicks. An adult was found dead at another box. Undaunted, the group erected another forty-four boxes the next summer.

"It was a miserable year," Elsie recalled. "Five pairs of bluebirds used the boxes, and a total of eleven fledged, but we found so many of the adults dead." Some fell victim to cats, the most widespread predator. Elsie took several puzzling cases to veterinarians at Oregon State University. She learned that some of the bluebirds had picked up intestinal parasites by eating pillbugs (*Armadillidum vulgare*), hard-shelled isopods introduced from Europe.

Gradually, young bluebirds hatched at successful

Elsie Eltzroth marks young bluebirds with distinctive combinations of small colored bands; thus she can recognize the birds without recapturing them. Her observations of mate selection, nest sites, and longevity have added to the store of knowledge about western bluebirds. (Photo copyright by Connie Toops)

nest boxes began to spread to new locations. In 1992, nearly four hundred baby western bluebirds fledged.

Elsie and her crew of thirty volunteers shift into high gear each spring. They have placed more than a thousand nest boxes within a twenty-five-mile (40-km) radius of Corvallis. Two hundred of the most productive are monitored weekly, beginning at nest-building time in early April.

Elsie tries to visit each active bluebird box two or three times during the nesting season. (Photo copyright by Connie Toops)

Volunteers keep records of each visit. They report to Elsie the dates eggs are laid and when the young hatch. She stops by active boxes two or three times during the nesting season. Since 1981 Elsie has placed numbered aluminum bands on the legs of baby bluebirds before they leave the nest. She also adds one, two, or three thin plastic bands in color combinations unique to each bird. When she sees a bluebird later, she zooms in with her spotting scope to record its band colors. In good light, she also reads the tiny numbers on the metal band. By consulting her records, she can identify the bird without recapturing it.

Elsie knows the genealogies of her bluebirds better than many people know their family trees. Most bluebirds in her study area remain within five miles (8 km) of the box where they were raised. Several, however, have been recovered thirty to sixty miles (48–96 km) away.

At one box on her rounds, a discussion between Elsie and volunteer Jorjie Coakley sounded like a script from a soap opera. "This is the second year for this female at this box," Elsie learned after squinting through her scope. "She lost her mate last summer, but a banded immature male from a site five miles [8 km] away joined her and helped raise the babies. He became her mate this year."

Elsie was especially interested in this box because she had placed an orphan in it. The foster parents adopted it in addition to their five babies. But the orphan's wing was damaged. If it could not fly, Elsie would eventually take it home to join the three permanently disabled bluebirds she cares for. One perky male, named "Robin Hood" because he came from Sherwood, Oregon, accompanies Elsie to schools when she presents programs.

Another male bluebird that was color-banded and released near Elsie's mountainside home has returned for brief visits, even though her house is not in prime bluebird habitat. He stopped by twice during the summer of 1991 and once in 1992. Early in 1993 he brought a mate. He usually sits on the TV antenna, chirping to the handicapped birds in her outdoor aviary. For Elsie, it is as gratifying as a child returning home on a break from college.

Elsie typically drives two thousand miles (3,200 km) and donates countless hours observing bluebirds each season. She can't think of a better way to spend her time. "My life is taking care of the bluebird kids after my own kids left the nest," she quips.

Human Champions

Earlier in the twentieth century, farmers, orchardists, and birders realized that the appealing "blue robins" they loved so dearly were disappearing. A few individuals began to promote bluebird conservation by building nest boxes. Among the most active and outspoken was Dr. Thomas E. Musselman of Quincy, Illinois.

Musselman witnessed an exceptional storm in 1895, when three weeks of snow and sleet covered foods vital to returning eastern bluebirds. "Bluebirds died by the thousands," he later wrote. As time passed, Musselman noticed there were fewer orchard and fence post nest sites available, with increasing numbers of house sparrows and starlings competing for them.

"The thought occurred to me," Musselman stated in a 1934 article in *Bird-Lore* magazine, "that if the House Wren population could be increased so materially by the erection of bird-houses, perhaps the Blue-birds would likewise respond." Musselman experimented with several designs during the 1920s and 1930s. "Almost every box of the mail-box type which I attached low down on a fence-post rewarded me with a first and later a second nest of Bluebirds," he explained. "They prefer a plain box with a single hole as entrance."

Musselman sent plans for nest boxes to area schools and by the mid-1930s encouraged bird-lovers to put up "a battery of several hundred Bluebird boxes placed at well-selected points throughout the country." These later became known as bluebird trails. Magazines and newspapers publicized Musselman's plans, and his idea of bluebird trails gained popularity throughout Illinois.

Dr. Oliver Austin maintained a bird-banding station on Cape Cod in the early 1900s. He put up five hundred nest boxes around North Eastham, Massachusetts. Most were used by tree swallows and bluebirds. Beginning in 1936, Amelia Laskey placed five dozen nest boxes in parks in Nashville, Tennessee. She monitored the nesting success of eastern bluebirds there for several decades. William Duncan maintained a large bluebird trail in Jefferson County, Kentucky, during that era.

In 1938 a coalition of garden clubs, birders, and the Missouri highway department recognized their state bird by creating the National Bluebird Trail. (Missouri is one of four states with the bluebird as its ambassador. New York also claimed the eastern bluebird, while Nevada and Idaho chose the mountain bluebird.) By 1946 the trail included 6,728 boxes, but bluebirds declined and interest gradually waned.

❧

Hubert Prescott was one of the first western bluebird champions. He grew up near orchards in southern Oregon and, prior to World War II, worked as an entomologist in Portland. During this time, Prescott enjoyed watching western bluebirds, which were fairly common throughout the foothills, orchards, and ag-

The idea of placing trails of nest boxes for bluebirds in rural settings gained popularity in the early 1900s. (Western bluebirds, photo copyright by Hugh P. Smith, Jr.)

Above left: A female western bluebird peers from a nest box originally constructed by Hubert Prescott. (Photo copyright by Connie Toops) Above: Minnesotan Dick Peterson designed an angled nest box that may help avoid blowfly infestations while repelling cats and raccoons. (Photo copyright by Connie Toops) Left: Little did Larry Zeleny realize, when he installed the first nest box at the Beltsville Agricultural Research Center in Maryland, that he was beginning a crusade to save eastern bluebirds from extinction. (Photo copyright by Connie Toops)

ricultural areas of the Willamette Valley. After a six-year absence, Prescott returned to Portland in 1951. He was dismayed to no longer find western bluebirds in the area.

Upon retirement, Prescott recalled seeing his last bluebird about 1945, "in a bird house on a barn located in the northern end of the valley." He used his spare time to search for them, and on Chehalem Mountain in July 1971, he finally glimpsed a western bluebird on a utility wire. As he watched, it ducked into a nest box mounted on an old shed. From the property owner, Prescott learned of four neighbors who also maintained bluebird boxes. He believed the remnant population had potential to grow, so he returned with more nest boxes.

In the following decade, Prescott constructed nearly 1,500 bluebird houses. Members of the Portland Audubon Society helped install some of them, and Prescott spent countless hours observing bluebirds. By the late 1980s, he witnessed a slow but steady increase in the numbers of western bluebirds in the northern Willamette Valley.

Canadians also noted declines in bluebird numbers during the middle of the century. In 1955 Charles and Winnifred Ellis of Lacombe, Alberta, began setting out nest boxes for mountain bluebirds. Three years later, John and Norah Lane of Brandon, Manitoba, organized the Brandon Junior Birders to build boxes and monitor nests. The idea spread from town to town. Eventually their dream of bringing bluebirds back to the prairies led to nearly five thousand nest boxes along 1,500 miles (2,400 km) of roads. Stuart and Mary Houston of Saskatoon, Saskatchewan, and Lorne Scott of Indian Head, near Regina, Saskatchewan, were major contributors. Scott, who began building nest boxes as a high school student in 1963, added about two hundred new boxes annually. In 1968 his trail met that of the Brandon Junior Birders in Broadview, in eastern Saskatchewan. The Houstons' trail linked with this network, expanding it to the northwest.

The Canadian Prairie Bluebird Trail now stretches 2,500 miles (4,000 km) from Winnipeg, Manitoba, to North Battleford, Saskatchewan. It includes some seven thousand boxes and fledges between five and eight thousand bluebirds annually.

In southern Alberta, Duncan Mackintosh

founded Mountain Bluebird Trails in 1974. The Edmonton Natural History Club, Harold Pinel and the Calgary Field Naturalists Society, and the John Janzen Nature Center have distributed tens of thousands of nest boxes during the past two decades. Work begun by Charles and Winnifred Ellis continues as Ellis Bird Farm, a center for conservation of bluebirds and other native cavity nesters. The center's research and educational programs are supported by Union Carbide.

Primary beneficiaries of trails in central Canada are mountain bluebirds. The Ontario Eastern Bluebird Society and La Société des Amis du Merle Bleu d'Amérique (Bluebird Society of Quebec) promote eastern bluebird conservation. Affiliates of Mountain Bluebird Trails in British Columbia host both mountain and western bluebirds.

~

The crippling late winter storm of 1958 caused observers to mourn "droves" of starving eastern bluebirds. The following spring, George J. Wallace and his students at Michigan State University found just two eastern bluebirds in the region. One nest box proprietor reported an active nest. That fall Wallace drove 1,668 miles (2,684 km) on Michigan's back roads. In twelve days he counted ten eastern bluebirds. Their future seemed bleak.

About the same time, Dick Peterson, who grew up in good bluebird habitat near Clarissa, Minnesota, observed declines in the area west of Saint Cloud. He felt a safer house with a design tailored to the bird's needs might help. Peterson noticed female bluebirds nested in the corners of square boxes with spacious floors. He tried an angled bottom, necessitating a smaller nest. He found a serendipitous bonus. "With the smaller bottoms, there were fewer blood-sucking blowflies," Peterson recalled. He believes blowflies lay eggs in proportion to space near the bottom of the nest. His boxes often contain a tenth the fly larvae of those with larger floors.

Peterson angled the roof to make it harder for cats or raccoons to sit on the box and catch a bird. He also analyzed how adult bluebirds entered boxes with round holes and decided an oval hole would be superior. Ovals allow adults to tip their heads and shoulders in to feed nestlings quickly without entering the box. With properly sized entry holes, small-floored Peterson boxes are not attractive to starlings, although they do occasionally squeeze in. House sparrows will enter, but live traps can be inserted to catch them easily.

Peterson's box is the most common design in the region, thanks to promotion by the Minnesota Department of Natural Resources and the Bluebird Recovery Program. Tens of thousands of these boxes dot the north-central states and Canada. Generations of bluebirds have accepted Peterson's efforts and imprinted on the inverted A-frame shape as home.

≈

Another champion of eastern bluebird recovery is a slightly built, modest man who hails from Minnesota. His name is Larry Zeleny. Larry spent much of his professional life as a biochemist, studying cereal grains at the eight-thousand-acre (3,200-hectare) Beltsville Agricultural Research Center near Washington, D.C. One of his most significant contributions, however, began accidentally.

When I visited with Larry at his home in Hyattsville, Maryland, in the spring of 1993, he recalled the incident. "One day in the early 1960s," Larry remembered, "a coworker of mine noticed a pair of bluebirds in the branches of some oak trees outside her window at the main building of the center. She called me over from my office on the second floor to have a look."

"I've made houses for bluebirds since I was fourteen years old. I put up the first one in Minneapolis in 1918. In those days it was fairly common to see bluebirds, even in the city," Larry said. "At the center, prior to 1950, bluebirds were still common. But in the 1960s, seeing bluebirds there was unusual."

"I speculated that if we put up a house, they might nest," he continued, "but we needed permission from the superintendent of grounds. Within about thirty seconds this woman called and obtained it. That was on a Friday afternoon."

Larry constructed a nest box on Saturday and installed it the next morning at the side of the building, facing a grassy lawn. The bluebirds began building their nest on Monday. Larry realized the center's scattered trees and numerous cross-fenced pastures provided an ideal place for bluebirds. By the time he retired in 1966, he had more than sixty nest boxes positioned around the complex.

Bluebirds became Larry's passion. Every Sunday morning during the nesting season, he made his rounds, evicting house sparrows and checking on the bluebirds' progress. Zeleny banded bluebirds for a number of years. He also studied tree swallows, which took a liking to the boxes.

Larry shared his knowledge—notes on foods, courtship, nesting, predator guards, comparisons of box designs, tips on raising orphaned bluebirds—in regular articles for birding newsletters. He helped establish about seventy-five bluebird trails that fledged nearly four thousand young by the mid-1970s. Based on these experiences, Zeleny wrote *The Bluebird: How You Can Help Its Fight For Survival*, which has been studied by countless hopeful bluebird hosts. In 1978 he formed the North American Bluebird Society (NABS), which fosters bluebird conservation.

NABS currently boasts 4,500 members in the United States, Canada, and Bermuda. They maintain about 47,350 nest boxes. In 1992, 11,773 of those were used by bluebirds. Larry believes NABS plans publicized in magazine articles, newspapers, and conservation mailings may be responsible for an additional 400,000 nonmembers putting up bluebird houses.

In Zeleny's living room, I was surrounded by pictures of bluebirds and other cavity nesters, a nest box made into a clock, and stacks of books on bird-related topics. At age eighty-nine, Larry's failing eyesight no longer allows him to monitor the bluebird trail. His friend Tom Valega, a bat conservationist, has taken over the route. Tom chauffered us five miles (8 km) from Larry's home to the center, where we found bicyclists and joggers enjoying a quiet spring morning on the huge farmstead.

Both men checked the first box, in which a house sparrow sat on a rambling nest with five speckled eggs. Since the center has numerous barns, cattle, and sheep, sparrows are abundant. "Monitoring is very necessary here," Larry commented. "Male sparrows go into the boxes and peck the heads of young bluebirds until they kill them," he said. "They even kill the adults."

Tom grabbed the sparrow. Turning away, he wrung

her neck, then dropped the limp bird into a plastic bag. He explained, "I'll feed this to an injured screech owl I'm caring for."

Farther along, Tom installed a new box he hoped would give bluebirds a fighting chance against sparrows. It featured a long front entry with space for the nest at the rear. "In theory," he said, "a bluebird on the nest could rush at, and perhaps repel, a sparrow that tries to enter the box. Traditional designs allow the sparrow to drop on top of the startled adult or defenseless young." Larry, who tested many box designs and predator guards here, was curious about the new style. He asked Tom to keep him informed of its success.

We continued down farm lanes, stopping every quarter mile (0.4 km) or so to check a box. One in four had a sparrow nest. About half contained bluebird nests or eggs. Larry recalled, in most years, two of every three boxes attract bluebirds. Seventy to 80 percent of them fledge chicks. Last year, 1992, was the most successful. Each box occupied by bluebirds produced young.

We did not find any house wrens. I asked Larry if that was unusual. "I had one Carolina wren on this trail," he answered, "but I've never had a house wren. My box at home has numerous wrens. They're attracted by the shrubs. I suppose it's too open here for them."

Zeleny added, "They're not the villains some people make them out to be. I like to watch and hear them. But it's best to locate bluebird boxes in open areas. Let wrens have the shrubs."

The sun was directly overhead as we checked the final box. We encountered numerous adult bluebirds on the fences and utility wires. Many boxes had a full complement of five eggs or young. I mentioned to Larry that the first time I saw all the bluebirds at the center, I got goose bumps thinking about how this spot has been a nucleus for their recovery. Bluebirds fostered here have expanded throughout the mid-Atlantic region.

Larry was reluctant to dwell on his successes, but with a modest smile, he replied, "I do think about

that now and then. It's given me lots of pleasure. I know there were very few bluebirds out here before I started putting up these boxes."

Zeleny estimated eastern bluebird populations decreased by 90 percent between the 1930s and 1970s. Audubon Christmas Bird Counts and U.S. Fish and Wildlife Service records indicate their recovery was slow at first. Eastern bluebird populations were low during the 1960s. They increased a bit in the early 1970s, but gains were wiped out by extreme winters in 1977 and 1978. Since then, according to Bruce Peterjohn, coordinator of the Fish and Wildlife Service Breeding Bird Survey (BBS), "Eastern bluebird populations have shown gradual, fairly consistent increases."

Data collected on about two thousand BBS routes in the United States and Canada indicate eastern bluebirds have increased at the average annual rate of 6.1 percent from 1982 through 1991. Some of the largest regional gains took place in the Upper Midwest. In Bermuda, where urbanization has obliterated most of the natural nest sites on the twenty-square-mile (52-square-km) island and introduced starlings and house sparrows rival bluebirds for cavities, a population of about a thousand eastern bluebirds persists. They depend completely upon nest boxes maintained by human hosts.

Mountain bluebirds increased at the average annual rate of 2.7 percent in North America from 1982 through 1991. They have multiplied in the Prairie Provinces and the Great Basin but have decreased along routes in the Southwest, California, and British Columbia. Western bluebirds have decreased in North America from 1982 to 1991 at the annual rate of 2.0 percent. Populations along routes in Colorado, Montana, and Washington have increased, but they are offset by decreases along BBS routes in Arizona, California, and Idaho.

As we parted company, Larry Zeleny, still an eloquent spokesperson for his birds, made a request. "Mention in your book that bluebirds need people," he said. "Without concerned people putting up and monitoring nest boxes, the bluebirds won't survive."

Above: *Hubert Prescott realized western bluebirds had nearly disappeared from the northern Willamette Valley by the middle of this century. He located a remnant population and put up a number of bird houses to increase their nesting success. A network of dedicated volunteers has continued the project since Prescott's death. (Male western bluebird, photo copyright by Connie Toops) Top inset: Tom Valega and Larry Zeleny place an experimental bluebird nest box on the grounds of the Beltsville Agricultural Research Center. (Photo copyright by Connie Toops)*

Bottom inset: *House sparrows frequent barns, such as those at the Beltsville Research Center, where they feed on grains and livestock wastes. Sparrows evict bluebirds from nest boxes and fill them with rambling nests. Monitor Tom Valega removes the speckled house sparrow eggs to give bluebirds another chance to use the box. (Photo copyright by Connie Toops)*

Bluebird Trails

A Cross-Country Sampler

Newberg, Oregon

During the 1970s, Hubert Prescott placed hundreds of nest boxes for western bluebirds in the northern Willamette Valley. He was assisted by members of the Portland Audubon Society, including Earl Gillis, a teacher from Newberg, and Pat Johnston, a nurse from Portland. Along with Brenda McGowan, also a nurse and Audubon member, Gillis and Johnston continued trail maintenance after Prescott's death. Through numerous educational programs, they have enlisted area residents to monitor nest boxes near their homes.

The terrain southwest of Portland is hilly, capped by a 1,500-foot-high (457 m) basalt ridge that extends for fourteen miles (22.5 km) along Parrett and Chehalem mountains. The land supports a mix of suburban homes, vineyards, and small farms that grow filberts, blueberries, and blackberries. Ten to 25 percent of the nest boxes here are occupied by western bluebirds. Many of the remainder are claimed by tree and violet-green swallows. Pat and Brenda visit the active boxes on a regular schedule and try to band all of the young bluebirds before they fledge.

When I toured part of the trail with Pat Johnston, she carried a tub of mealworms along with her banding equipment. "First nestings in this area can be disasters,"

she told me. "We tend to get good weather in late April and early May when the bluebirds begin to nest. Then we usually have a cold, wet period around Memorial Day when adults have trouble finding enough food. Many of our monitors put out mealworms to assist the adults," she explained. She left a handout of the straw-colored larvae on the ground or on top of each box she checked. Bluebirds recognize the monitors and wait patiently while they look into the boxes. As soon as the monitor leaves, the birds swoop in excitedly for their treat. They carry four or five mealworms at a time in their beaks as they fly to feed nestlings.

Pat pointed out a nest box at Pleasant Hill Cem-

Pat Johnston inspects a western bluebird nest box located at the edge of a vineyard on Chehalem Mountain. (Photo copyright by Connie Toops)

Brenda McGowan checks the band on a male western bluebird. (Photo copyright by Connie Toops)

etery. The following day I returned with Brenda McGowan, who banded the birds. "This nest is the lowest elevation we know of so far," she explained. "Usually western bluebirds don't nest below five hundred feet [150 m] in this region, but this is the second pair we have found at around two hundred feet [61 m]. We hope this is a result of an expanding population."

Brenda used mealworms to entice the female into a wire cage. She checked her band and determined the bird fledged nine miles (14.5 km) away on Chehalem Mountain. Moments later she captured and banded the male. Then she gently removed seven fuzzy babies from the box and banded them. "This is the second nest of seven raised here this year," she said. As she worked, we heard young bluebirds, probably the first brood, calling from the woods at the edge of the cemetery.

Next we drove to the home of Jim and Janet Harvey, the young couple whose box fledged the female now nesting at the cemetery. "You're bluebird grandparents," Brenda announced as we arrived. The Harveys, whose nest box is mounted on the deck railing, sorted through snapshots to find a picture of the 1990 brood. As they reminisced, they recalled what happened at the same box the following year.

"The female disappeared when the babies were about three days old," Janet remembered. "The male would feed the five little ones mealworms, but he couldn't brood them. Brenda has used pocket hand warmers to keep babies warm in remote boxes. Since this was so close to the house, Harv rigged up a soil-warming heat strip inside the box and plugged it in right here."

"Everything was fine," she continued, "until a cold, wet night when the heat strip came unplugged. When we found the listless babies the next morning, we thought they were dead. So into the trash can they went."

"Brenda stopped by that morning," Janet recalled. "We told her about the tragedy, and she commented she had once revived some cold babies by placing them on a hot water bottle."

"Of course," Jim interjected with a grin, "Brenda was kind enough to accept the word of an anesthesiologist and a cardiac RN that these bluebirds were really dead. As soon as she left, we rushed to the trash can and found, miracle of miracles, three of the 'dead' babies were moving."

"We warmed them with a hair dryer," Janet continued, "then Harv put them in a baby incubator we happened to have. In the meantime, the male was frantically searching around the box for his babies."

"So we called Brenda," Jim recounted, "and she brought a nestling from another box to decoy the male. He continued to visit the nest. By the next morning, two of the little ones were strong enough to put back. We fed the remaining one in here every ten minutes. Finally it went back to the box, too, and all three fledged. We even saw them coming back to the feeder and looking in the box later that year."

Passing the Hammer

Aretirement-aged bluebirder commented to me, "Bluebird trails fade as old ladies die."

It is tragic when an elderly monitor has no one to take over her or his bluebird trail, but it does not happen often. Those who know the joy of bluebirds cannot imagine life without the familiar flash of blue and the friendly chortles of these gentle birds. They also realize the importance of introducing youngsters to bluebirding.

One of these energetic youth leaders is Betty Nichols. I found her on a breezy May afternoon in Middletown, Maryland. She was surrounded by six boys and an advisor from Scout Troop 476. They were looking curiously at a broken bird egg.

Betty became aware of the plight of bluebirds in the late 1970s. She established bluebird trails on her farm and at a nearby cemetery. Later she received permission from the Frederick County Bureau of Parks and Recreation to install a trail skirting grassy recreational fields near Middletown High School. Scouts accompany Betty on her weekly monitoring route to earn merit badges.

When everyone had arrived, we headed to the nearest nest box. Several of the boys rode ahead on bicycles, but according to Betty's instructions, they approached cautiously and waited for us to catch up to open the box. The first nest contained five white eggs, which Betty explained were somewhat unusual.

Two of the scouts jumped across a creek to inspect a box on the opposite side while the rest of us walked uphill to a house where a female tree swallow crouched. Betty showed the boys the feathers the swallow used to insulate her nest. We skirted the baseball diamond and looked at a nest that previously contained three bluebird eggs. Now it held only one, cold and splattered with yolk. The box was located close to shrubs. Betty theorized that a house wren drove the bluebirds away. As the scouts approached box 5, they spotted a male bluebird on guard duty. The female flushed as they opened the lid, revealing five warm eggs. They looked briefly, then retreated so the parents could return.

Tree swallows occupied two more boxes. Finally Betty peeked into a formerly vacant box at the far end of the park. She began waving her arms, enthusiastically calling the scouts closer. "It's a new bluebird nest," she exclaimed. "See, the male and female are sitting on the wires over there." With Betty's help, the boys calculated the time it would take the eggs to hatch. "Good," one of them announced, "that's before school is out. We'll get to see the babies."

Later that summer, Betty called to tell me about her successful bluebird fledglings. She added proudly, "You know, I gave a nest box to one of the scouts who was helping me. His mother says he has been more interested in bluebirds than any other project he's done. He takes people on tours at the park, but he makes sure they don't disturb the birds too long. It's wonderful to see kids of that age interested in birds."

Nest box trails are an excellent means to pass the legacy of bluebirds to future generations. (Photo copyright by Connie Toops)

Although bluebirding projects are now popular among many youth groups, the Camp Fire organization was among the first to promote bluebird awareness. This is especially appropriate since young participants in Camp Fire are called Bluebirds. In 1971 advisor Mary Janetatos brought bluebird conservation to her local Camp Fire group through camping experiences for children and workshops for leaders. These activities evolved into Project Save the Bluebirds, in which Camp Fire girls nationwide built and monitored nest boxes.

About the same time, Chuck Dupree, then grounds manager at Goddard Space Flight Center in Greenbelt, Maryland, invited Camp Fire groups to place nest boxes on portions of that facility managed to benefit wildlife. A few years later, Janetatos and Dupree helped organize the North American Bluebird Society.

Many schools have adopted bluebirds as class projects. In Austin, Texas, environmental science teacher Ken Lightle guides students at Bowie High School in studying bluebird behavior, the birds' place in the food chain, and predator-prey relationships. They maintain 132 nest boxes on the large school campus and along a nearby bicycle path. This is a cooperative project involving the city, the school, and a private real estate development. In January the class repairs or rebuilds nest boxes for the coming season. Each student monitors five, keeping a weekly journal of nesting activity and problems such as parasites or predators.

Lightle hopes to evoke appreciation for the environment. "Many of these students are from the city, and they may not have spent lots of time outside," he explained. "This can be an emotional experience for everyone involved. When we gently pick up a nesting female to check eggs, it may be a student's first time touching a live bird. When fire ants invade boxes, we've had tears as students realize how fragile life is."

Lightle's students also host workshops for elementary classes. They show the bluebird trail to the younger kids, then help them build nest boxes to take back to their schools. In six years of the program, Lightle has seen local interest intensify. Parents and neighbors have put up bluebird houses in their own yards, and bluebird sightings are increasing in the area.

Richard Tuttle first learned about bluebirds as a youngster on an Ohio farm. Now as a teacher of middle school life science, he blends bluebird trail management into the curriculum. Tuttle's students learn about habitat, bluebird life histories, carrying capacity, and competition. They also build nest boxes, which many maintain around their homes as they grow to adulthood.

Many state nongame wildlife programs offer workshops to help residents construct bluebird nest boxes. In Hutchinson, Minnesota, a conservation club has hosted similar workshops for children for the past seven years. Lumber is donated and precut by volunteers. When the kids arrive, they and their parents put the boxes together. According to Dave Ahlgren, who has attended to provide information on choosing a successful box site, the 1993 workshop had been enthusiastically promoted on television. "Normally they have about three hundred children participating," Ahlgren commented, "but this was a beautiful spring day. About 550 kids arrived with a parent in one hand and a hammer in the other."

The club had forty volunteers ready to help the kids, but they realized 350 sets of box parts would not be enough. Luckily Dale Kenning had started to cut out boxes for the following year's workshop. "The sheriff was there," Ahlgren continued, "so with red lights flashing, he escorted some helpers as they rushed to Dale's farm and loaded up more box parts."

"In the meantime, they also ran out of hot dogs and buns to feed the kids," Dave said, "so they canvassed the town for more food. When they returned, they even had a donation of one woman's homemade bread. Of course, the TV crew documented the whole affair."

Carrol Henderson, director of Minnesota's nongame program, knows the workshops are worthwhile. When he initially gave seminars in the early 1980s, he asked if anyone had seen a bluebird. "Older people said they saw them when they were children," he reported. Now when Henderson visits schools and nature centers, a majority of hands go up in response

Above: *Workshops hosted by conservation clubs and state game agencies invite youngsters to join in the hobby of bluebirding. (Photo copyright by Connie Toops)* Right: *Various schools have adopted bluebird trails. Students learn woodworking skills when they make or repair nest boxes and gain an appreciation for the environment as they watch bluebirds at their nests. (Photo copyright by Connie Toops)*

to the same question. In 1993, Minnesota Bluebird Recovery Program members tallied 12,171 eastern bluebird fledglings leaving their boxes. That figure is about ten times the number fledged a decade ago.

≈

In his *National Geographic* article, Larry Zeleny described bluebird trails as a "network of hope." A score of years later, Zeleny's wish for bluebird success is being realized. I doubt, however, that Larry envisioned the full impact bluebirds would exert on the lives of the dedicated individuals who maintain nest boxes for them.

Thousands of people have discovered that a relatively small investment can return bluebirds to a prominent place in our lives. Yes, it takes time to make the boxes and to hike or drive the trails, monitoring and checking them. But bluebirding is a hobby unrestricted by age, gender, or educational background. It provides a rewarding opportunity for young and old to learn about and protect a fascinating aspect of our environment. To the monitors, bluebirds are not just symbols. They become friends. The birds provide an excuse to spend quality time outdoors, enjoying nature and exploring new places. They lead to a lifestyle that combines mystery and adventure with deep satisfaction.

Several decades ago this precious link to our wild heritage nearly disappeared. Now, through education and active conservation practices, we can pass the legacy of bluebirds to future generations.

Among the pleasant surprises of monitoring a bluebird box might be the discovery of an albino chick in a nest of chirping babies. (Eastern bluebirds, photo copyright by Michael L. Smith)

Welcoming Bluebirds
to Your Yard

"Bluebird conservation," wrote Larry Zeleny, "offers an unusual opportunity for people who are truly concerned about our wildlife heritage to accomplish something by means of direct action. . . . to do something tangible, to become directly involved, in an activity that will help save some valuable species of wildlife from annihilation."

That may explain why farmers, homeowners, and folks from all walks of life have collectively mounted an estimated half-million bluebird houses along the fencerows and back roads of North America. It is hard to be personally involved in saving an endangered species such as a manatee or a rhinoceros, but many of us can have a pair of bluebirds if we are willing to modify our backyards slightly. In so doing, we become managers of personal refuges. Just as proprietors of state or national wildlife lands, we must address three basic considerations: shelter, food, and water.

Shelter

Bluebirds are accepting of various designs for nest boxes. I have seen them successfully nesting in boxes of plastic, plywood, pine, and cedar, with oval, circular, or slot entrances, mounted on trees, pipes, posts, and buildings. A few of the variations are dictated by the birds' needs. Most are expressions of box-makers' preferences. Is the pattern simple to cut out and put together? What materials are readily available? Have several generations of birds imprinted on this style and thus recognize it as "home?"

This book includes nest box plans from several regions. You may have excellent success with the simplest or a local favorite. If not, try another type. You can seek help reading the plans or cutting the parts at a wood shop class at your nearest vocational school. When deciding upon the style of box to construct or purchase, you will want to address seven considerations.

Materials. Wood is reasonably priced, easy to work with, and durable. Pine is readily available and least expensive, though it warps as unfinished surfaces weather. Western red cedar has natural rot resistance and does not require painting. Plywood is also quite serviceable, although new sheets give off formaldehyde fumes. Allow new plywood boxes to season before mounting them.

Plans in this book are sized for "inch lumber," which is actually 3/4-inch thick (1.875 cm) Thinner wood does not insulate nests well enough. Wooden boxes are most secure when screwed together or constructed with glue and nails. Boxes constructed with staples may fall apart as they weather. Pine and plywood can be painted a light color or treated with several coats of linseed oil to help weatherproof them.

Bluebirds help us to become personally involved in protecting wildlife in our own backyards. (Photo copyright by Connie Toops)

Do not paint or coat interior surfaces. Do not use copper-arsenate treated lumber (recognized by its greenish color) for houses or feeders.

Concrete and pottery bird houses are fairly well insulated, but they are heavy to mount and awkward to open for monitoring.

Plastic jugs make inexpensive nest cavities, but unless they are covered with several coats of light paint, temperatures inside will be too hot for successful nesting. Houses made of PVC pipe heat and cool more slowly than wood. They may deter house sparrows. Check to see how easily they open for monitoring.

Cardboard may be an inexpensive material, but birdhouses made of waxed cardboard do not provide adequate insulation or predator proofing. Do not use them.

Dimensions. The height from the floor of the box to the bottom of the entrance hole should range from 5 to 7 inches (12.7–17.8 cm). The minimum floor space needed for eastern bluebirds is 3½ inches by 3½ inches (8.9 cm x 8.9 cm) in Peterson boxes and 4 inches by 4 inches (10.2 cm x 10.2 cm) in rectangular boxes. Mountain and western bluebirds need floors measuring at least 5 inches by 5 inches (12.7 cm x 12.7 cm).

Perches. House sparrows and wrens readily use perches. They are not necessary for bluebirds or swallows. Roughen the wood inside, under the entrance hole, to assist birds when they exit.

How does the box open? Cleaning is easiest if the front or side swings open. If you plan to monitor the box regularly, it is easiest to peek in by lifting the lid. Mount the box so the nest cavity will be at eye level. Boxes that open from the bottom are unsuitable for monitoring.

The fastener should be easy to open, yet secure. In your yard, a hook or peg may suffice. If the box is in a high-traffic area, a screw is harder for casual passersby to remove. If you oversee several boxes, use the same type of fastener on each, so only one opening tool is needed.

Heat conservation and air conditioning. Small gaps between the sides of the box and the roof or holes drilled into the upper sides will ventilate the box in the summer. If bluebirds roost in the boxes in the winter, you may wish to plug the vents for additional warmth. A roof that overhangs the front by at least 2 inches (5.1 cm) will keep out rain or snow. A shallow saw kerf under the roof will keep rain from soaking into the box. Small holes in the corners of the floor prevent moisture from accumulating.

Ease of attachment. Consider where the box will be mounted and how it will attach. Waxed or greased metal poles are the best choice for repelling raccoons, snakes, and other climbing predators. Where predators are not prevalent, wooden posts may be satisfactory. Although nailing nest boxes to isolated trees seems to work well for bluebirds in the West, tree-mounted boxes in the East and South are prime targets for predation.

Box site. Bluebirds nest where they find abundant food. The most promising sites are sunny openings with short grasses or low vegetation. Suburban lawns, gardens, pastures, and old orchards are good choices. Avoid areas treated regularly with pesticides.

Mount the nest box in the open, a hundred feet (30 m) from dense woods or brushy areas. Bluebirds require lookouts, such as dead limbs or utility wires, from which to hunt for insects.

In hot climates, the entrance should face away from direct afternoon sun. In areas where rainy weather is prevalent, point the opening away from the direction of most storms. Although boxes with entrances near the bottom and perch pegs inside are advertised as winter roosts, bluebirds are more likely to use a winterized nest box that faces away from prevalent winter winds.

Food

Bluebirds do not eat the sunflower or thistle seeds many of us feed to chickadees, titmice, goldfinches, and other backyard birds. But bluebirds do supplement their insect diet with small fruits. Many of these grow on shrubs, vines, and trees that are attractive additions to home landscapes. Plantings and certain types of feeders will draw bluebirds to your yard.

Offer a variety of plants so berries will be available throughout the seasons. Mulberries and wild cherries ripen in time to be fed to fledglings. Dogwood and mountain ash are favorite foods of fall migrants. Holly and hackberry retain fruits late into the winter, and thus are helpful to bluebirds at a time when food is scarce. Fruits such as rose hips, in which flesh surrounds small seeds, offer more energy than sumac berries, which have little flesh and large, indigestible seeds.

Consult the "Landscaping for Bluebirds" section of this book, and seek advice at local garden centers to decide on species that will grow well in your yard. When adding trees and shrubs around your home, plant the tallest at the back of your property or along the rear edge of beds. Visualize their mature height, and arrange them so they will not block windows or views. Place them so you can watch the birds as they feed.

As trees and shrubs mature, you may wish to shape them by pruning. Freeze or dry clusters of berries that you remove and offer them as food later in the winter.

If bluebirds visit your backyard regularly, you may be able to entice them to a feeder near a window. Bluebirds frequent solid, rather than swinging, feeders. Choose a location safe from cats and other predators. The birds may find the feeder on their own, or you may need to place food near their natural hangouts, then gradually move it closer to your house.

A berry feeder is a simple way to draw a bluebird's attention. Mount a board or piece of plywood on a post. Drill about two dozen small holes through the wood. Clip fruit clusters from bluebird-attracting trees or shrubs, and slip the stems into the holes in the feeder. In the winter you may wish to harvest clusters of rose hips or sumac fruits from roadsides or weedy fields where they grow in abundance. You can also purchase commercially harvested dogwood berries. These fruits keep well for a month or so when stored in a cool, dry place. Bluebirds readily visit feeders for them. Some people also successfully offer dried currants or chopped raisins.

The bluebird equivalent of ice cream must be a mealworm. These inch-long (2.5-cm), cream-colored creatures are larval darkling beetles, which are pests at commercial grain elevators. They are sold in bait and pet shops but are less expensive when purchased directly from suppliers in larger quantities.

Mealworms survive for several months when kept in a cool, aerated container of wheat bran with an apple or potato slice added for moisture. Eventually the larvae molt into sluggish white pupae, which bluebirds also relish. Adult beetles lay eggs that grow into more mealworm larvae. It is easy to culture mealworms yourself, and children enjoy the project of growing them.

Many proprietors of bluebird nest boxes keep mealworms handy from late winter through the nesting period. In cold, wet weather, when the birds have difficulty finding insects, offer a handful of mealworms in a small plastic lid nailed to the top of the box or placed nearby on the ground. The birds catch on quickly. They gobble up the offering, stuffing as many as half a dozen in their beaks before entering a nest box to feed hungry babies. Do not drop mealworms into the nest box. Let parents decide when and how many mealworms to feed their offspring.

Mockingbirds, woodpeckers, nuthatches, and starlings also relish mealworms, and sometimes claim them before bluebirds do. Some bluebirders have success with roofed, Plexiglas-sided feeders that have entrance holes sized for bluebirds. The Plexiglas allows bluebirds to see food inside, but sometimes inexperienced birds become confused. They try to exit through the clear panels instead of the holes. Use black tape or an indelible marker to create a pattern on the Plexiglas. If bluebirds seem reluctant to enter such a feeder, try removing a panel or the roof until they are more comfortable. A few bluebirders have conditioned their birds to come for mealworms when they whistle or ring a little bell.

Is it possible to feed bluebirds too many mealworm treats? Caretakers at zoos and wildlife rehabilitation centers agree that mealworms are high in protein content, especially if they are allowed to consume some dry dog food the day before they are offered to the birds. But mealworm larvae are encased in a hard exoskeleton that is not easily digestible. It traps protein inside. Adult bluebirds select softer larvae and pupae when they are available. Before feeding mealworms to their babies, they often whack the larvae against a hard surface to rupture the exoskeleton. But I have seen adults gulp down six to eight mealworms in a row without cracking them open. There is some question whether these worms are adequately digested. To be safe, supplement a bluebird's diet with mealworms but encourage it to hunt natural foods that will provide balanced nutrition.

Although bluebirds are not as likely to eat grains, some people successfully offer concoctions that contain peanut butter, suet, cornmeal, flour, or sunflower hearts. A popular recipe is listed on page 122. These mixtures can be packed into holes drilled in logs or crumbled onto a shallow feeding tray. Refrigerate the mix so the suet will not turn rancid. Offer small amounts at a time and replace food dampened by rain or snow so it will not spoil.

Water

Another simple way to attract bluebirds is providing a safe, reliable water source. Bluebirds drink and bathe frequently in the summer and require drinking water throughout the winter. A shallow birdbath or bowl of water about an inch (2.5 cm) deep is perfect for bluebirds. It should be large enough for the whole family to enter together if they wish. Chickadees and many other songbirds simply splash water droplets onto their feathers. Bluebirds immerse, fluttering their wings and tails briskly and dipping their heads under water for a thorough soaking.

❧

Nearly a century ago, naturalist John Burroughs wrote, "How readily the bluebirds become our friends and neighbors when we offer them suitable nesting retreats."

Bluebird hosts are creative and resourceful people. I have traveled nearly five thousand miles (8,000 km) across the United States, visiting back-yards and farmsteads groomed to attract these joy-fully addictive birds. No two trails, no two nest boxes have been exactly alike.

Bluebirds allow us to become inventors and im-provers. We try a new box site, we tinker with a latch or a predator guard. We experiment with a new feeder or a better birdbath. And the bluebirds? They buoy our spirits by poking their heads in the box to size it up, by sampling a bit of the newest food recipe, or simply by perching within our view and momentarily making our world a better place.

There is more to the hobby of bluebirding than mounting a box on the back fence and forgetting about it. Lifting the lid to peek into this fascinating realm brings anticipation, surprises, and occasional disappointments. The bluebirder's reward for convert-ing yards, farms, or adopted sections of trail is pride—knowing that these places are now graced by the gentle presence of bluebirds.

Above: *Bluebird houses fashioned from PVC pipe may not be as attractive to house sparrows as traditional wooden nest boxes. (Photo copyright by Connie Toops)* Oppo-site top left: *Although special roosting boxes with holes near the bottom have been designed for them, bluebirds are more likely to use regular nest boxes as winter roosts. (Photo copyright by Connie Toops)* Opposite top right: *Mount nest boxes at least a hundred feet from brushy ar-eas. Face the openings away from the direction of most storms and shade them from the afternoon sun. (Photo copyright by Connie Toops)* Opposite bottom: *Many bluebirders offer mealworms during cold, wet weather when the birds might have trouble finding enough food for themselves or their babies. (Female western bluebird, photo copyright by Connie Toops)*

Top inset: *Bluebirds will frequent a feeding platform that holds clusters of fruit, such as wild grapes, rose hips, or dogwood berries. (Photo copyright by Connie Toops) Bottom inset: Bluebirds enjoy frequent baths in warm weather. (Eastern bluebird, photo copyright by Gregory K. Scott)*

Above: *Place the birdbath in a spot where cats would have difficulty hiding in ambush. (Photo copyright by Gregory K. Scott)*

Landscaping for Bluebirds
Plants that attract eastern bluebirds

Trees with fruits available in summer or fall

black gum (tupelo)	*Nyssa sylvatica*
buckthorn, Carolina	*Rhamnus caroliniana*
cherry, black	*Prunus serotina*
cherry, pin	*Prunus pensylvanica*
chokecherry	*Prunus virginiana*
dogwood, flowering	*Cornus florida*
mulberry, red	*Morus rubra*
mulberry, white*	*Morus alba*
serviceberry, downy	*Amelanchier canadensis*

Trees with fruits available in winter

hackberry	*Celtis occidentalis*
hawthorn, Washington	*Crataegus phaenopyrum*
holly, American	*Ilex opaca*
mountain ash, American	*Sorbus americana*
red cedar, eastern	*Juniperus virginiana*
sugarberry	*Celtis laevigata*
winterberry, smooth	*Ilex laevigata*

Shrubs and herbs with fruits available in summer or fall

blackberry/raspberry	*Rubus* sp.
blueberry	*Vaccinium* sp.
dogwood, alternate-leaf	*Cornus alternifolia*
dogwood, red-osier	*Cornus stolonifera*
elderberry, American	*Sambucus canadensis*
lilyturf*	*Liriope muscari*
pokeberry	*Phytolacca americana*

Shrubs and herbs with fruits available in winter

bayberry	*Myrica pensylvanica*
blackhaw	*Viburnum prunifolium*
chokeberry, red	*Aronia arbutifolia*
cotoneaster, small-leaved*	*Cotoneaster microphyllus*
firethorn*	*Pyracantha coccinea*
holly, Foster*	*Ilex x attenuata 'Fosteri'*
juniper, common	*Juniperus communis*
mistletoe	*Phoradendron serotinum*
rose, multiflora*	*Rosa multiflora*
sumac, smooth	*Rhus glabra*
sumac, staghorn	*Rhus typhina*
sumac, dwarf	*Rhus copallina*
viburnum, cranberry	*Viburnum trilobum*
wax myrtle	*Myrica cerifera*

Vines with fruits available in summer and fall

grape, wild	*Vitis* sp.

Vines with fruits available in winter

bittersweet, American	*Celastrus scandens*
grape, winter	*Vitis vulpina*
poison ivy	*Rhus radicans*
Virginia creeper	*Parthenocissus quinquefolia*

*nonnative

Opposite: *Eastern red cedar (Juniperus virginiana). Opposite inset: Male eastern bluebird with mulberry. (Photos copyright by Connie Toops)*

Main photo: *Dogwood* (Cornus florida) *in autumn*. Top inset: *Male eastern bluebird on feeder stocked with rose hips and dogwood berries*. Bottom inset: *Rabbit-eye blueberry* (Vaccinium ashei). Opposite inset: *Foster holly* (Ilex x attenuata 'Fosteri') (*Photos copyright by Connie Toops*)

Landscaping for Bluebirds
Plants that attract western and mountain bluebirds

Trees with fruits available in summer or fall

buckthorn, cascara	*Rhamnus purshiana*
cherry, bitter	*Prunus emarginata*
chokecherry	*Prunus virginiana*
dogwood, Pacific	*Cornus nuttallii*
mulberry, white*	*Morus alba*
serviceberry, common	*Amelanchier alnifolia*

Trees with fruits available in winter

California pepper tree*	*Schinus molle*
hackberry	*Celtis occidentalis*
holly, American	*Ilex opaca*
juniper, Rocky Mountain	*Juniperus scopulorum*
juniper, western	*Juniperus occidentalis*
madrone, Pacific	*Arbutus menziesii*
mountain ash, European*	*Sorbus aucuparia*

Shrubs and herbs with fruits available in summer or fall

blackberry/raspberry	*Rubus sp.*
blueberry	*Vaccinium sp.*
currant	*Ribes sp.*
dogwood, red-osier	*Cornus stolonifera*
elderberry, blackbead	*Sambucus melanocarpa*
elderberry, Pacific red	*Sambucus callicarpa*
fig, common*	*Ficus carica*
lilyturf*	*Liriope muscari*

Shrubs and herbs with fruits available in winter

coralberry	*Symphoricarpos orbiculatus*
firethorn*	*Pyracantha coccinea*
holly, Foster*	*Ilex x attenuata 'Fosteri'*
juniper, common	*Juniperus communis*
mistletoe, dwarf	*Arceuthobium pusillum*
rose, wild	*Rosa woodsii*
snowberry	*Symphoricarpos albus*
sumac, smooth	*Rhus glabra*
viburnum, cranberry	*Viburnum trilobum*
winterberry	*Ilex verticillata*

Vines with fruits available in summer and fall

grape	*Vitis sp.*

Vines with fruits available in winter

bittersweet, American	*Celastrus scandens*
moonseed	*Menispermum canadense*
poison oak	*Rhus diversiloba*
Virginia creeper	*Parthenocissus quinquefolia*

*nonnative

Opposite: *Wild blackberries* (Rubus *sp.*). Opposite inset: *Male western bluebird.* (*Photos copyright by Connie Toops*)

Bluebird Banquet
© 1992 Linda Janilla

1 cup peanut butter
1 cup zante currants
4 cups yellow corn meal
1 cup small sunflower chips
1 cup rendered suet, melted
1 cup peanut hearts
1 cup flour

Mix well. Mixture will be granular, but will stick together. If too sticky, add more cornmeal. Refrigerate until use. Pack into feeder log or crumble on tray to serve.

Main photo: *Firethorn* (Pyracantha *sp.*). Top inset: *Smooth sumac* (Rhus glabra). Bottom inset: *Rocky Mountain juniper* (Juniperus scopulorum). *(Photos copyright by Connie Toops)*

References

Avise, J. C., J. C. Patton, and C. F. Aquadro. 1980. Evolutionary genetics of birds. *Auk* 97:135–147.

Aylesworth, A. 1987. Mountain x western bluebird hybrids. *Sialia* 9:9,21.

Bent, A. C. 1949. *Life histories of North American thrushes, kinglets, and their allies.* U.S. National Museum Bulletin No. 199. Washington, D.C.

Boone, J. E. 1984. Bluebird posture: understanding bluebird behavior. *Sialia* 6:137–143.

Borland, H. 1975. Wildlife in the promised land. *National Wildlife* 13(6):24–25.

Brawn, J. D. 1984. Defense of nest boxes by western bluebirds during the post-breeding period. *Condor* 86:494–495.

Cary, J. 1993. The secret lives of birds. *National Wildlife* 31(4):38–45.

Darling, C., and J. Thompson-Delaney. 1993. Bluebirds, blowflies, and parasitic wasps. *Sialia* 15:13–16.

Dion, A. P. 1981. *The return of the bluebird.* St-Placide, Quebec: Editions Auto-Correct-Art.

Eltzroth, E. K. 1983. Breeding biology and mortality of western bluebirds near Corvallis, Oregon. *Sialia* 2:67–71.

——, and S. R. Robinson. 1984. Violet-green swallows help western bluebirds at the nest. *Journal of Field Ornithology* 55:259–261.

Gillis, E. 1989. Western bluebirds, tree swallows and violet-green swallows west of the Cascade Mountains in Oregon, Washington and Vancouver Island, British Columbia. *Sialia* 11:127–130.

Goldman, P. 1975. Hunting behavior of eastern bluebirds. *Auk* 92:798–801.

Gowaty, P. A. 1981. The aggression of breeding eastern bluebirds towards each other and intra- and inter-specific intruders. *Animal Behavior* 29:1013–1027.

——, 1983. Male parental care and apparent monogamy among eastern bluebirds (*Sialia sialis*). *American Naturalist* 121:149–157.

——, A. A. Karlin, and T. G. Williams. 1989. Behavioural correlates of uncertain parentage: mate guarding and nest guarding by eastern bluebirds, *Sialia sialis*. *Animal Behavior* 38:272–284.

Gower, C. 1936. The cause of blue color as found in the bluebird and the blue jay. *Auk* 53:178–185.

Graber, R. R., J. W. Graber, and E. L. Kirk. 1971. *Illinois birds: Turdidae.* Biological Notes #75, Illinois Natural History Survey. Urbana, Illinois.

Grooms, S., and D. Peterson. 1991. *Bluebirds!* Minocqua, Wisconsin: NorthWord Press.

Grussing, D. 1978. How do you get rid of sparrows? *National Wildlife* 16(2):10–13.

Harrison, G. H. 1992. Is there a killer in your house? *National Wildlife* 30(6):10–13.

Henderson, C. L. 1992. *Woodworking for wildlife.* St. Paul: Minnesota Department of Natural Resources.

Hensley, R. C., and K. G. Smith. 1986. Eastern bluebird responses to nocturnal black rat snake nest predation. *Wilson Bulletin* 98:602–603.

Herlugson, C. J. 1983. Growth of nestling mountain bluebirds. *Journal of Field Ornithology* 54:259–265.

Kaufman, K. 1992. The practiced eye: bluebirds. *American Birds* 46:159–162.

Laskey, A. R. 1951. Effect of the 1951 ice storm on bluebird nesting. *Migrant* 22:42.

Low, J. 1992. Tips on birdhouses. *Birder's World* 6(2):50–54.

Manry, D. E. 1992. The mating game. *Birder's World* 6(4):16–21.

Martin, A. C., H. S. Zim, and A. L. Nelson. 1951. *American wildlife and plants: a guide to wildlife food habits.* New York: McGraw-Hill.

Munro, H. L., D. H. Munro, and R. C. Rounds. 1981. Fertility of albinistic eggs of mountain bluebirds. *Auk* 98:181–182.

Musselman, T. E. 1934. Help the bluebirds. *Bird Lore* 36:9–13.

Peterson, R. T. 1992. Introduced species. *Bird Watcher's Digest* 14(6):12–19.

Pierson, T. A. 1977. Bluebird numbers in Virginia as determined from Christmas bird counts, 1945–1975. *Raven* 48:75–76.

Pinkowski, B. C. 1971. Some observations on the vocalizations of the eastern bluebird. *Bird-Banding* 42:20–27.

——, 1974. A note on familial longevity in eastern bluebirds. *Bird-Banding* 45:363–364.

——, 1975. Yearling male eastern bluebird assists parents in feeding young. *Auk* 92:801–802.

——, 1978. Five years of observations of a male eastern bluebird. *Jack-Pine Warbler* 56:161–163.

——, 1980. A montage of defiants—ten accounts of unusual bluebird behavior. *Sialia* 2:19–21.

Pitts, T. D. 1978. Eastern bluebird mortality at winter roosts in Tennessee. *Bird-Banding* 49:77–78.

——, 1984. Historical population changes of eastern bluebirds in northwest Tennessee. *Sialia* 6:43–47.

Power, H. W. 1980. On bluebird cuckoldry and human adultery. *American Naturalist* 116:705–709.

——, 1980. Male escorting and protecting females at the nest cavity in mountain bluebirds. *Wilson Bulletin* 92:509–511.

——, 1989. The long hot summer of '88: bluebirds liked it hot. *Natural History* 98:61.

——, 1989. Birds of song and lore. *Birder's World* 3(4):14–18.

Prescott, H. W. 1983. Ash-throated flycatchers and plain titmice compete for bluebird nest boxes in Oregon. *Sialia* 5:123–124.

——, and E. Gillis. 1985. An analysis of western bluebird double and triple nest box research on Chehalem and Parrett Mountains in 1982. *Sialia* 7:123–130, 146.

Preston, F. W., and J. McCormick. 1948. The eyesight of the bluebird. *Wilson Bulletin* 60:120–121.

Sauer, J. R., and S. Droege. 1990. Recent population trends of the eastern bluebird. *Wilson Bulletin* 102:239–252.

Schutsky, R. M. 1980. Helping behavior of the juvenile eastern bluebird. *Sialia* 2:91–93.

Scott, L. 1971. Male eastern bluebird assists female mountain bluebird in raising young. *Blue Jay* 29:126–127.

Scriven, D. H. 1989. *Bluebird trails: a guide to success.* Minneapolis: Audubon Chapter of Minneapolis.

Shalaway, Scott. 1992. Nest box fever. *Wildbird* 6(3):48–51.

Simpkin, J. L., and A. A. Gubanich. 1991. Ash-throated flycatchers (*Myiarchus cinerascens*) raise mountain bluebird (*Sialia currucoides*) young. *Condor* 93:461–462.

Stokes, D., and L. Stokes. 1990. Helpers at the nest. *Bird Watcher's Digest* 12(6):105.

——, *The bluebird book: a complete guide to attracting bluebirds.* Boston: Little, Brown and Company.

——, Attracting spring bluebirds. *Wildbird* 7(3):58–61.

Tuttle, R. M. 1982. Livestock guards make bossie, black beauty, and bluebirds compatible. *Sialia* 4:65–69.

——, 1987. A study of winter roost site management and the use of sites by eastern bluebirds in Delaware State Park, Delaware, Ohio. *Sialia* 9:43–49.

——, 1990. Details for a front opening bluebird nest box with a slot entrance. *Sialia* 12:13–17.

——, 1991. An analysis of the interspecific competition of eastern bluebirds, tree swallows, and house wrens in Delaware State Park, Delaware, Ohio, 1979–1986. *Sialia* 13:3–13.

——, 1991. Eastern bluebirds nest over water. *Sialia* 13:83–87.

Wallace, G. J. 1959. The plight of the bluebird in Michigan. *Wilson Bulletin* 71:192–193.

Welty, J. C. 1968. *The life of birds.* New York: Alfred A. Knopf.

Zeleny, L. 1976. *The bluebird: how you can help its fight for survival.* Indiana University Press, Bloomington.

——, 1977. Song of hope for the bluebird. *National Geographic* 151:854–865.

Zickefoose, J. 1993. *Enjoying bluebirds more.* Marietta, Ohio: Bird Watcher's Digest Press.

Index

About the Author

Connie Toops grew up in the small town of Covington, in west-central Ohio. She attended Ohio State University, earning a Bachelor of Science degree in natural resources in 1972. While in college she spent the summers working as a seasonal naturalist in the Ohio state park system and in Colonial, Rocky Mountain, and Shenandoah national parks. Later she worked as a naturalist and ranger at Everglades, Shenandoah, and Crater Lake national parks.

Now a freelance photojournalist, Connie writes articles that appear regularly in conservation magazines. Her photos have graced Audubon and Sierra Club calendars and books published by National Geographic, the Sierra Club, Reader's Digest, Time-Life, and Voyageur Press. She has written nine nature books for adults, including four other Voyageur Press titles: *The Enchanting Owl*, *Great Smoky Mountains*, *Everglades*, and *Hummingbirds: Jewels in Flight*. She also has developed and written the *Let's Explore* series of children's nature activity guides.

Connie and her husband Pat, a resource management specialist for the National Park Service, have lived in or near seven national parks and monuments during the past two decades. They share a love of birding, canoeing, and other outdoor activities, and have explored parks, preserves, and natural areas throughout the United States and in Belize, Mexico, and Australia. They currently make their home in Martinsburg, West Virginia, where they are landscaping a suburban half-acre into a mini wildlife refuge.